Beyond Bristol

24 Country Walks

Robin Tetlow

 *redcliffe*

First published in 2017 by
Redcliffe Press Ltd.,
81g Pembroke Road, Bristol BS8 3EA

 redcliffepress redcliffepress

Reprinted October 2017

info@redcliffepress.co.uk
www.redcliffepress.co.uk

© text and photographs: Robin Tetlow; cover painting: Yvonne Tetlow (1916-2014);
cover design: Stephen Morris

ISBN 978-1-911408-14-7

British Library Cataloguing-in-Publication Data
A catalogue record for this book is available from the British Library

Design and typesetting by Stephen Morris www.stephen-morris.co.uk Set in Goudy 10/12
Printed in the Czech Republic via Akcent Media Ltd

The Walks

Introduction

As well as attracting ever increasing numbers of tourists and visitors, greater Bristol is a highly desirable and fashionable location in which to live and work. Perhaps one of the more underestimated of the many assets of the area is its easy access to countryside of outstanding quality and diversity.

My aim is to guide you towards enjoying the best of this countryside. Over the past 30 years I reckon to have completed more than 300 different walks in the locality. The 24 walks in this book are quite simply my favourites. All are within easy reach of Bristol, all are serious walks and all should be within the capabilities of most people.

Who is the book for?

• Are you looking to get fitter and healthier? Perhaps you are not entirely enthused by a trip to the gym or a bike ride or other available options? The physical and psychological benefits of regular walking are becoming increasingly recognised. This book aims to show you that a half or a full day escape into the countryside is an ideal antidote to stressful everyday life. Walking is both healthy and enjoyable.
• Perhaps you have lived in the Bristol area for a while but have never fully explored the countryside beyond Bristol? Or maybe you have only recently moved to the area or are visiting it? The Mendips, the Cotswolds, the Somerset Levels, the Severn Estuary and the Wye Valley are all within easy reach; and there is a great deal more to explore besides. Most of the walks have additional historic and natural interest.
• Or maybe you are a keen and active walker who knows the countryside beyond Bristol, and are looking for a compilation of the best half-day and full-day walks? This may save your having to plan your own routes or at least assist you in continuing to do your own.

How have I chosen the 24 walks?

The selection is inevitably subjective. However, each of the walks does fit within the following broad framework:
• All the walks are easily accessible from the centre of Bristol – that is no more than 25 to 30 miles or one hour away by car.
• The length of each walk is within the range of 6 miles to 11 miles. The length is intended to be sufficient to justify a special trip to the start and to ensure some serious exercise. Similarly the achievable time for each of the walks is in the range of 3 hours to 6 hours.
• As far as possible the walks traverse the highest quality landscapes, and incorporate as many features of historical, archaeological and natural interest as possible. As country walks as far as possible they avoid busy roads and other noisy distractions.

- I have aimed to select a representative range and variety of walks across the whole of area.
- I also acknowledge the inspiration and influence of other, now out of print publications produced over the past 30 years, most notably several by Sue Gearing and Geoff Mullett.

Please note the following about the format of the book and the guidance given for each of the 24 walks:

- Comprehensive written instructions are given for each of the walks. I have done each of them many times and at different times of the year. However, conditions vary greatly through the seasons – for example, conditions underfoot will tend to be muddier between November and March.
- The text for each walk explains the route in detail and is complemented by an OS extract showing the route and some key stages along it. Please note, however, that these maps are not reproduced to their original scale. Therefore, it may be advisable to carry with you the identified OS Explorer 1:25.000 map.
- Estimated distances are provided; shorter distances on the walks are in metric only.
- Estimated walking times have been provided for each walk but of course your actual time will depend not only on the conditions and your pace but also how frequently you choose to stop to view the various features and/or for refreshments.
- This is first and foremost a walking book. The emphasis is on ensuring that you find your way round the route. The description of the features and scenery is economical. So, whilst most of the walks incorporate features of special natural, historical or archaeological interest, I often simply point them out without much detail. It is reasonably easy to delve further if you want.
- Car parking suggestions are made for each of the walks. For some there is generous dedicated car parking at or near to the start; for others the options are more limited and you may have to look beyond the immediate locations I have suggested. Please always park sensibly and considerately.
- Some of the walks are accessible by public transport and I would encourage this option if available. However, in view of all the variables it is only realistic to leave you to do your own investigations.
- Refreshment options are listed for each of the walks. Neither their availability nor their quality have influenced the selection of the walks. I strongly suggest that you check all the relevant details, such as opening times, in advance.
- I have done my best to provide up to date and accurate information on each of the routes. I have carefully checked each of the routes in the very

recent past. My checks have confirmed, though, that changes will inevitably continue to occur from time to time. Fortunately most should be minor, such as gates replacing stiles. Apologies in advance if I have not been as clear as I should.

• This book is designed to enable you to escape from the stresses of modern technology, so it does not specifically cater for following the routes via your mobile phone. Your phone should be taken for use in an emergency though.

• All these walks are suitable for many occasions, at different times of the year and in a range of different conditions. Above all it is for you to enjoy the various features of these walks in your own way.

I offer the following further additional advice based on my experience of completing each of these walks on many occasions:

• Be realistic about your fitness and capabilities. There is a range of walks in this book; ultimately all should be within the capabilities of anyone who is reasonably fit and active. However, if you have not done much walking before you may need to build up your fitness first by doing some training walks in your locality. Otherwise you could start with some of the shorter and gentler walks in the book and progress from there.

• Wear stout shoes/ankle-high walking boots with socks for all walks in all conditions. Protect your legs – I would not recommend shorts even in the hottest of conditions. Avoid jeans, especially in wet conditions.

• Walking poles are very helpful, particularly on those walks including steeper gradients. I now take a single walking pole with me on every walk – they can have other uses, such as in clearing away brambles.

- Check the weather forecast the day before and on the day of the walk and take account of anticipated conditions in your preparation.
- Take a rucksack. Regardless of conditions and intended refreshment stops, it will always be sensible to carry with you your mobile phone, some food, some drink (about a litre) and plasters; and to have in reserve waterproofs, gloves and layers of clothing.

Please ensure that you keep to the **Natural England Countryside Code** but expect others to do so as well. See:
www.gov.uk/government/publications/the-countryside-code

The key elements for walkers are:

- Be safe, plan ahead and follow any signs.
- Leave gates open or closed as you find them, use gates, stiles or gaps when they are provided and do not climb over gates or fences unless necessary.
- Protect plants and animals and take your litter home.
- Keep dogs under close control.
- Consider others.

I trust that you will enjoy completing, and regularly repeating, these walks as much I have. If you do then please join the **Ramblers Association**, the national organisation which exists to promote the interests of walkers and walking, particularly in maintaining and improving footpaths. On many of the routes you will see that local groups have directly contributed to waymarking and to the provision of new gates and stiles. Local groups also organise regular walks. See **www.ramblers.org.uk**

Finally, may I thank my immediate family, Dina, Lara and Justin for their help and inspiration throughout this project.

Hawkesbury and Hawkesbury Upton

Distance 6 miles / 9.5 kms

Time 2.5 to 3 hours

OS Map Explorer 167

Starting Point Village hall car park, High Street, Hawkesbury Upton - OS Reference 773870

Parking Free village hall car park

Reaching the start from Bristol Go east on the M4. Leave by Junction 18 and then go north on the A46. After about five miles take the left turn to Hawkesbury Upton. The car park is in the High Street, on the right just beyond the Beaufort Arms

Refreshments Beaufort Arms, Hawkesbury Upton

THE FIRST WALK in the book is an ideal primer. Not only is it the shortest walk in the book but one of the least strenuous, albeit with a couple of testing climbs. Perhaps more importantly the coombes, meadows and lanes of the Cotswold countryside provide superb scenery. Walking is mainly on tracks and well-defined footpaths. There are muddy sections.

The walk starts in the village of Hawkesbury Upton. From the northern edge of the village the route descends into Upton Coombe and then continues along Small Coombe. After passing through the hamlet of Lower Kilcott, along a quiet country lane, you follow the Monarchs Way up Long Coombe and through woodland. Beyond here there are panoramic vistas, including across the Severn Estuary and beyond, as the walk circles in the direction of the medieval village of Hawkesbury. From the village the path climbs Church Hill to pick up the Cotswold Way, from which there are views of the Hawkesbury Tower. Upon re-entering Hawkesbury Upton you pass an ancient pond, before returning to the High Street.

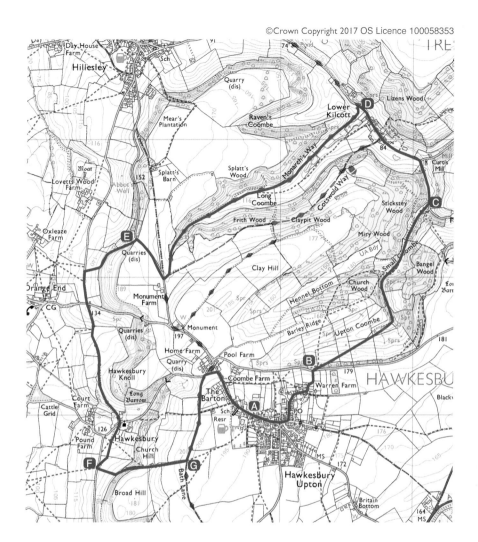

©Crown Copyright 2017 OS Licence 100058353

A From the village hall car park, turn left along the High Street for 200 metres until you reach the war memorial. Here turn left and then left again along Back Street. Stick with this road as it deviates right and left out of the village. Pass Warren Farm on the left and ignore a waymarked track straight ahead of you as the road bends to the left. After exiting the village the road eventually reaches a T-junction. Cross the road to the signed footpath opposite.

B Take the path and descend via a copse and through a gate. Continue ahead on a track down and across the next three fields via a series of field gates. On entering the fourth field look out for a footbridge down to your left. Head down towards this to cross the stream and reach a track. Turn right on the track and now follow the stream on your right along the valley. Continue on the track with the stream next to you on your right for about a further 600 metres. Keep along the broad valley bottom, which may be muddy, until

tom. Here the track joins up with a path that emerges from the left. Continue with the track as it curves around to the right and gradually climbs up the valley. Carry on up the field as far as you can, as it funnels towards a field gate straight ahead. Go through the gate to enter woodland. Climb steeply up the stony track. Upon exiting the woodland you reach a T-junction of tracks, at which the Hawkesbury Monument is clearly visible ahead. Turn right at this junction to soon reach the main road. At the road junction turn right along the road for about 300 metres. Proceed with care and use the uneven verge where possible. Cross the road at the brow of the hill to reach a footpath off to the left.

E Upon entering the field ignore the first gate you see off to your left. Instead take a less obvious gate about 20 metres beyond. Go through this gate into another field and turn right. Keep to the right-hand field boundary and follow it downhill for about 200 metres until you reach a gate off to the right. Take the gate and go down steps and through a further gate. Then head straight across the field to take a stile on to a lane. Turn left and proceed along the lane until you reach a T-junction. Immediately ahead of you is a field gate. Go through the gate. Continue on the track ahead as it undulates and meanders in the direction of Hawkesbury village. Very soon after going through another field gate the church tower comes into view. Continue on the track to descend in the direction of the church. Upon reaching the village go ahead through a gate and cross a lane to reach the perimeter of the church. Pass the churchyard wall on your left, to take a stile into a field. In the field keep with the graveyard wall and then head for the field gate straight ahead. Go through this and head towards another field gate in the far right-hand corner of the next field.

you reach a crossing track which goes over the stream. Here take the bridge to cross the stream and continue with the stream now on your left. Head for a field gate, which you can see ahead.

C Go through the gate and turn left along the lane. Keep with the lane as it skirts woodland and curves round left. Pass Corn Mill Farm on the right. Ignore the waymarked Cotswold Way track off to the left. Continue along the lane for about 250 metres beyond here, passing a further footpath off to the left and various properties off to both the left and right. When you reach a large pond on your right look out for a footpath sign opposite off to the left.

D Cross the stile and follow the track as it curves uphill with the left-hand boundary. As the terrain levels out, continue ahead with the track towards a field gate/stile. Cross the stile and in the next field keep with the track and the left-hand boundary as it now descends with two ponds on the left. Descend all the way to the valley bot-

F Go through the gate and on to the hedged and surfaced track. Turn left to climb steeply up the track. Keep with the track as it meanders and passes through woodland. When you emerge from woodland continue uphill with the fenced track, as it goes through two field gates. The next field is more open. Keep uphill with the left-hand hedge to reach a field gate. Go through the gate to reach a T-junction with another track.

G Turn left, and proceed on the surfaced track, with the Hawkesbury Monument ahead of you on the horizon. With Hawkesbury Upton village off to the right, stay with this track all the way until you reach a gate leading on to a road.

H At the road turn right to reach a green and an ancient drover's pond immediately ahead. Pass the pond to reach the road junction. Turn right to pick up the pavement. Proceed uphill to join the High Street of Hawkesbury Upton. You will shortly reach your starting point, the village hall car park, on your left. **A**

Buckland Dinham and Mells

Distance 10.5 miles / 17 kms

Time 5.5 to 6 hours

OS Map Explorer 142

Starting Point High Street, Buckland Dinham - OS reference 754512

Parking Free on the High Street or by St Michael and All Angels Church

Reaching the start from Bristol Take the A37 south out of Bristol. Go through Pensford and Clutton. At Farrington Gurney take the A362. Continue on the A362 through Midsomer Norton and Radstock. From Radstock stick with the A362 and continue in the direction of Frome until reaching the centre of Buckland Dinham

Refreshments Talbot Inn, Mells or Bell Inn, Buckland Dinham

THIS IS A very varied walk combining some of the best countryside of the eastern Mendips with historic villages, railway paths, riverside walks, parkland, woodland and industrial archaeology. The terrain is mainly level but there are a couple of uphill stretches towards the end. There are some muddy sections.

The walk begins at the village of Buckland Dinham and soon picks up a green lane, with spectacular views of surrounding countryside plus also the remains of a disused colliery. The route then proceeds along a disused railway track and through a concrete works. From here the walk emerges again into attractive countryside centred on the prominent church tower of Mells. From the medieval village of Mells you continue for a considerable distance along the riverside of Mells Stream, passing a variety of industrial archaeology including the former Fussells' Ironworks and evidence of the never completed Dorset and Somerset Canal. From the valley the walk climbs through the Orchardleigh Estate, with distant views into Wiltshire, before passing via woodland and fields back towards the attractive vista of Buckland Dinham.

A Look out for the bus shelter on the same side of the High Street as the church. Take the footpath immediately opposite which runs immediately adjacent to Hill House. Follow this out to the full southern extent of Buckland Dinham. Immediately before the footpath heads out into open countryside via a gate, turn sharp right along a footpath behind the houses. Continue, to take a stile on to a road which you cross to pick up a track straight ahead.

B Continue on this hedged track in the same direction and gently uphill for about a further 1500 metres. After passing the remains of Oxley's Colliery on the left, of which the chimney is the most prominent remaining feature, Hill House Farm appears ahead. You eventually pass this on your left. Cross the driveway and continue ahead uphill for a further 150 metres before reaching a field gate. Go straight ahead through the gate and follow what is now a path along the right of the field to a stile in the hedge ahead. Cross this and enter a long field. Here keep to the left hand boundary as the path initially continues to climb but eventually moves downhill. Stop upon reaching an opening on the left, about 50 metres from the bottom of the field. At this point, strike out at 45 degrees across the field keeping to the lower slopes of the field. Head towards an often hidden stile in the middle of the boundary hedge ahead. Cross this stile, a track and a further stile immediately ahead at the end of the hedge line. The next field is also a long field. Follow the waymarked path along the field, keeping generally towards the upper slopes and the right of the field. On approaching the far boundary look out for some water standpipes. From here curve round left with hedge on your right for about 100 metres before reaching a concealed path in the hedge (very easily missed). Take this path and follow it through scrub up to the road. Turn left downhill on the road and continue until just after crossing the old railway bridge.

C Here you turn right on to the Colliers Way path, which you follow for a total of about 1500 metres. About 300 metres after passing beneath a bridge, and as a concrete works appears ahead, you reach a junction off to the right. Turn right to leave the railway path and then left at the minor road. Proceed gently uphill to a junction. Turn left over the bridge and continue for about 100 metres to another junction.

D Here turn left, following the footpath sign to enter the concrete works. The footpath signs through the concrete works are clear. After proceeding between the two main reception buildings, the key principle is to follow the path through the piles of concrete pipes and along the right hand boundary towards a stile in the far right-hand corner of the premises. Cross the stile back into open countryside. Proceed through two fields, crossing a stile and keeping to the right-hand boundary. Enter the following field via a field gate, with the landscaped grounds of Edney's Farm off to your left. Continue downhill along the right-hand boundary. Go through a field gate at the bottom. In the next field bear left uphill towards a small gate in the fence, proceeding past a pond off to your left. Go through the gate on to a drive.

E Cross the drive and immediately go through another similar gate. In the next field, proceed diagonally right towards the nearest telephone pole and then continue on this same line towards a stile in the corner. Cross the stile and proceed to the footbridge clearly visible ahead on

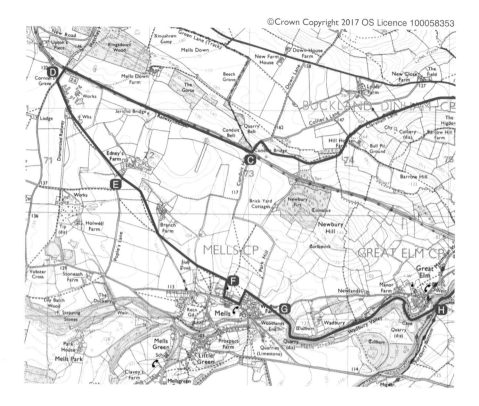

the far boundary. From the footbridge Mells church tower should now be visible. However, you initially take a line across the field well to the right of the church tower, towards a distinct clump of conifer trees. As you move towards and converge with the increasingly visible driveway off to your left, aim for a short stretch of wall directly ahead of you. You reach and cross the driveway just to the right of the wall. From the driveway now aim straight ahead across the large field towards Mells church tower. Keep to this alignment until you reach a gap in the hedgerow boundary. Enter the next field and now follow the track along the right-hand boundary hedge to the field corner. Here turn left and follow the path uphill towards a stile in the corner. Cross the stile. Follow a wall round to the right and cross a further stile to reach a field

adjacent to the churchyard. Take a stile in the wall to enter the churchyard.

F Proceed via an avenue of yew trees around the church and out of the churchyard into New Street, with the Talbot Inn immediately on the right. At the junction turn left along the road until you reach the war memorial on the left. Here take the road off to the left. Follow this road round to the right and, at the junction at the end, go across to enter a field. In the field initially follow the right hand boundary and then head towards the farm. On reaching the edge of the farm bear left towards and along the hedgerow. Continue along the hedgerow until you reach a stone stile by a telegraph pole off to your right. Go down to cross the stile and reach the road.

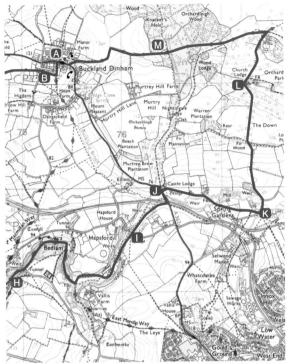

the footbridge ahead and then keep left with the path to shortly take a gate on to a road. You have now reached Great Elm, with a road bridge off to the left and an old mill pond ahead of you.

H Cross the road and proceed through the gate in the same direction, with the river still on your left and the railway on your right. Carry on under and beyond the railway bridge as the railway passes overhead. About 100 metres after passing a path off to the left go through the gate ahead and under a further railway bridge. Continue for a further 100 metres and then over a metal footbridge to cross the stream. At an immediate junction of paths fork right. Keep the river to your right until you pass two bridges in quick succession to reach an open area, off to the left. From here you continue with the river to your right to reach a high metal gate on the edge of an industrial area. Follow the fenced-in footpath around the outer perimeter of the industrial area and into it. Upon entry proceed towards the building immediately ahead and then turn right following the access road through a gate and out of the industrial area. After passing the Foxes Den Social Club on the right, look out for a metal staircase up an embankment. Take this and proceed to the top of the embankment into a copse. At the top stay within the copse. Take the left turn and proceed in parallel with the access road you have just left, all the way to steps leading down to the main road adjacent to the road junction.

G Walk left for 50 metres and then cross the road to pick up the wooded riverside path, leading off to the right. Follow the path with the river on your right. The remains of various derelict buildings next to the river soon appear off to the right. Within about 400 metres, you reach the most prominent of these, the former Fussells' Ironworks. Continue on past the ironworks along the riverside. Eventually the path merges with a hard surfaced driveway. Stick with this for 100 metres before forking off as directed on the well-defined riverside path. Continue until you reach a major pedestrian footbridge across the river. Turn right to cross the footbridge. Now continue in the same direction on the riverside path on the other side. Soon after houses appear over on the left, you reach a tributary river ahead. Deviate slightly to take

I Cross the road, go over the stile and stick with the clear footpath along the right-hand bank of the river. As you reach a disused aqueduct off to the left go through a gate. From here carry on with the river on your left until you reach another gate. Go through the gate and up a fenced footpath branching off to the right. With the railway now on your left follow the path up to a further gate and on to the main road. Go left over the bridge, keeping to the right hand side of the road, towards the main entrance of the Orchardleigh Estate ahead. Do not take this. Instead take the farm track to the right.

J Go through the gate and follow the fenced drive through open fields until reaching a cottage. Immediately opposite is a footbridge. Cross the footbridge and proceed ahead across the field to take a stile, a footbridge and a further stile across the stream. Here turn sharp left to follow the left hand boundary, initially alongside the stream and then up to and over an embankment carrying a driveway to cross a further stile. Bear right across the next field to take a stile in the far boundary. In the next field continue with the right-hand boundary to a further stile. Cross the stile, a driveway and a further stile. Cross the paddock towards a further stile in the right-hand corner, leading out on to a road. Turn left along the road, immediately ignoring two right turns. Continue with the road as it curves left to cross three river bridges in close succession, passing several houses, before reaching a stile and barrier ahead.

K Cross the stile and continue uphill through woodland keeping to the right-hand boundary until you eventually reach a stile leading into a field. Take the stile to enter the field. Continue with the field boundary to your right through two fields via a stile. At the end of the second field, go ahead through a gate and proceed uphill in the same direction across the open field towards a strip of woodland, looking out for a stile ahead. Cross the stile and follow the path in the woodland as it curves left and uphill. Soon the footpath becomes fenced. Continue on the fenced footpath as it directs you through two gates across a flat area that is now occasionally used as an airfield. There are views of nearby Orchardleigh House and (on a fine day) more distant panoramic views, including the Westbury White Horse. The path descends and exits on to a broader track which continues downhill towards estate buildings, with Orchardleigh Church 100 metres off to the right.

L From the junction with the driveway to the church, the track soon becomes a metalled lane. Continue past two estate houses and follow the lane uphill. You eventually enter a golf course. Follow the lane through the golf course until you reach a T-junction. Here turn left and after about 300 metres you reach an exit/cattle grid. At the exit immediately leave the road and head across grass, taking a route veering slightly away to the right. Go between two oak trees and head for about 200 metres in the direction of woodland ahead, with the road still no more than 75 metres away on your left and the edge of the woodland on your right. Look out carefully for a waymark post ahead at the point at which you should enter the woodland. Once in the woodland continue on the waymarked track, avoiding all turnings, including at a junction with farm buildings off to the left. Beyond here continue ahead and look out for when the track forks. Take the left turn fork. Proceed to descend to a stile on the far edge of the woodland.

M Go over the stile and exit into a field. As the church tower of Buckland Dinham appears on the horizon, keep down the right-hand field boundary. As the field narrows, go through the gate to pick up a short track. Go left into a further field. Head out diagonally across this field, initially in the direction of a lone tree in the middle. Beyond the tree continue on a line just to the left of Buckland Dinham church tower. Head towards the protruding field corner and then towards the gate/footbridge beyond. Go through the gate, cross the footbridge and through another gate to reach the final field. You continue to aim just to the left of the church tower. Proceed steeply up the field to a gate in the left hand corner. Go through this gate, up a track and through another gate. Pick up a walled path and then a driveway between walls. Exit the driveway next to the church. From here you simply turn left to reach the main road and the start of the walk. **A**

Doynton, Hinton and Dyrham

Distance 7.5 miles / 12 kms

Time 4 hours

OS Map Explorer 155

Starting Point Holy Trinity Church, Church Road, Doynton - OS reference 721742

Parking Free on-road parking at or near to the church

Reaching the start from Bristol Take the A420 out of Bristol. Continue through Warmley and Bridgeyate and through Wick to its furthest edge. Here take the left turn along Bury Lane, signed to Doynton and taking you to the village centre

Refreshments The Cross House, Doynton; the Bull Inn, Hinton; several seats on route for picnics

---

THIS WALK, set at the southern tip of the Cotswold Hills, comprises two contrasting halves. The first half is a leisurely stroll along the river between the pleasant villages of Doynton and Hinton. The second half is much more up and down, following the western escarpment of the Cotswold Hills along the Cotswold Way. There are extensive panoramic views south and west throughout this second half, and you skirt Dyrham House and Dyrham Park. Most of the walk is on well-defined footpaths and tracks; however there may be muddy conditions in the fields around the mid-point.

The walk progresses out of Doynton along the River Boyd through farmland and follows this for a considerable distance before deviating from the river across further farmland to the village of Hinton. From here, there is a steep climb up to Hinton Hill and Badminton Plantation, where the views begin to open up, soon followed by a steep descent to the village of Dyrham. You pass immediately by Dyrham House as you track the Cotswold Way via fields, copses and past ponds and up through Dyrham Wood. Upon exiting Dyrham Wood you leave the Cotswold Way, curving round the outside edge of the wood and steeply downhill to pass through fields and a green lane back to Doynton.

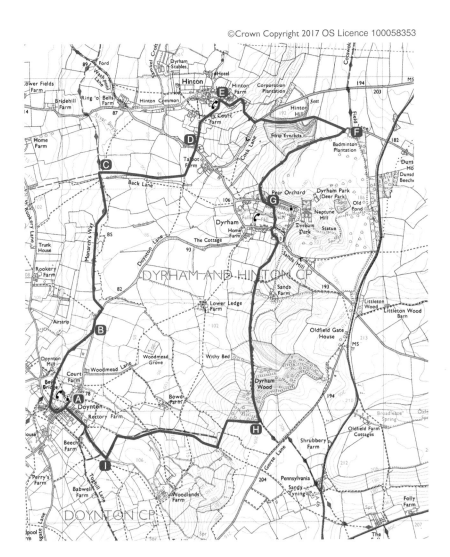

A From the church head back along Church Road to take the High Street, the first junction off to the right. You immediately pass the Cross House on the right and continue down the High Street for about 200 metres. When you reach the edge of the built-up area of the village, take the footpath signed off to the right leading up stone steps. Go through a gate to enter a field. Proceed diagonally down the field, keeping to the left of an electricity pole. Take a small stone bridge across a stream, ignoring a wooden footbridge across another stream over to your right. Go ahead through a gate in into another field, keeping Doynton Mill to your left. In the field proceed with the hedge on your left to take a stile in the left-hand corner. In the next field continue along the left-hand hedge for 50 metres until you pick up the River Boyd on your left – you will now be following this river for a considerable distance. Go through a gap into another field, and then across a small bridge over a tributary stream in the far hedge into a further field. In the further field, bear right to take a stile in the hedge and exit on to a road.

B Turn left on the road for about 200 metres, ignoring the first stile you see on the left. Shortly after this, turn left through a gate to take the path across a wooden sleeper bridge. Upon entering a field turn right and proceed ahead, with the River Boyd now on your right. After this, you pass via gates through a further four fields. The fourth of these fields is very long; at the end you go through a spinney via two closely spaced gates into a further field. About 50 metres into this field take the footbridge off to your right to cross the river and enter another field.

C You now head away from the river. Walk parallel with the trees on the right-hand boundary. Take a gate in the far boundary into another field. Proceed in a similar direction towards the right-hand corner of this field and through a gate in the corner. The conditions around the gates in this section of the walk can be very muddy. Proceed across the next field, taking your alignment on the farm buildings visible in the distance beyond. Go through a field gate in the far boundary. In the further field, go straight ahead in the direction of an electricity pole for no more than 75 metres. Then stop and bear sharply left, aiming for another electricity pole and between two buildings visible beyond the hedgerow. Head for a gate in the hedgerow, which you go through to reach a road.

D Cross the road to Chapel Lane. Walk along the full length of Chapel Lane. At the end pass a house on the left and then continue for 50 metres along a green stretch and through a gate into a paddock. Ignore the footpath signs directing you left; instead follow the right-hand boundary uphill. Continue up and across the field towards the top left-hand corner. Take a stile adjacent to the remains of a field gate to enter an overgrown field. With Hinton village ahead of you, veer right across this field to meet the corner of the hedgerow; then follow the left boundary along the field and descend to take a stile at the bottom, on to a road.

E Turn right on the road. You very soon reach the Bull Inn on your left. From here continue up the road. Climb steeply uphill and at the top, bear left with the main road, ignoring the junction off to the right. Within about 50 metres of the junction take a gate off to the right. Keep to the right hand edge of the field and follow the track downhill and along through scrubland as it goes around Hinton Hill. As you emerge from the scrubland into the open and you start to climb gently, the track becomes more of a green lane. Views open up of Dyrham Park and beyond down to the right. Continue ahead along the right-hand boundary, with a fort over to your left and through a gap into a field. Go down the field with hedge on your right and through a gate in the far boundary to enter a further field. Go up the field in the same direction, aiming for the centre of a clump of trees ahead on the horizon and then for a waymark post in front of a wall, which only becomes visible at close quarters.

F At the waymark you join the route of the Cotswold Way. Turn right to follow

the wall down the field boundary. Go through a gate into another field and continue to descend with the left-hand boundary, with impressive views both ahead and behind. Go through two successive gates and then down another field, and through a further gate to enter a small field. Cross this field towards woodland and through a gate to enter it. You pass a seat on the left before descending a sunken stony track to reach the village of Dyrham. Just before the road, you take a gate off to the left to follow a paved path through further woodland which runs parallel with it. The path soon emerges out on to the driveway of St Peter's Church, which is immediately adjacent to Dyrham House. Turn right and through a gate to exit the driveway on to the road. Turn left on the road and follow it gently downhill as it passes Dyrham House over to the left. Continue until you reach a small green and take the road off to the left. Proceed uphill for about 150 metres until you reach a footpath sign and gate off to the right, next to the main village sign.

G Go through the gap in the hedge, pass a seat under a tree and through a gate. Follow the fenced path alongside a hedge to your right. Go through a gate to enter a copse and a further gate to exit it. Keep ahead in the field over a crossing path, staying with the Cotswold Way. Go through a gate and through a further copse with a pond down to your left. Exit past a waymark post into a field. Go up and across the field. Exit through a gap in the far boundary. In the next field keep gently uphill with the left-hand boundary to pick up a track. Now descend on the track, still following the left-hand boundary to the field corner. Here, with a pond ahead to your right, take the gate ahead into another field. Head down the middle of the field and enter a copse. Cross a footbridge, go up some steps and then exit the copse via a gate into a field. Head steeply up the field in the direction of the woodland over to your left. Keep with the left-hand boundary towards the top left-hand corner of the field. Here take a gate to enter Dyrham Wood. Follow the path steeply uphill through the wood until you emerge via a stile into a large field.

H At this point, do not continue ahead with the Cotswold Way. Instead bear right. Keep uphill with the path curving around the outer edge of the wood. Stay with this path beyond the brow of the hill, as it bends further and descends quite steeply, with panoramic views ahead. At the bottom of the field, turn left and keep with the right-hand field boundary. Exit the field by a gate. In the next field keep ahead in the same direction and up the sloping field, with further woodland now over to your right. Continue for about 150 metres before reaching a crossing path and a stile in the fence on your right. Join the crossing path and take the stile, with Doynton visible in the far distance ahead of you.

I Go steeply down a long field towards it right-hand corner, with the same woodland over to your right. Go through a gate and then immediately left through another gate into another field. Continue straight down this field with the hedge on your right and go through a gate at the end. Continue down the next field likewise. Pass through a gate and across two bridges over a stream to enter a further field. Proceed gently up this field, still keeping to the right-hand boundary. Go through another gate and continue through a short field, which you exit via a gate towards the right-hand corner. You turn left to join a green lane. Although there is an obvious path ahead towards Dyrham village, continue left along the green lane. This eventually brings you out on to a surfaced lane, by St Ives Farm and a stream. Turn right to follow this hedged lane, Watery Lane, until you reach a road junction. With the recreation ground immediately ahead of you, turn right. This road takes you all the way back to a junction with Church Road, next to the church and the starting point. **A**

Westonbirt, Tetbury and Shipton Moyne

Distance 8.5 miles / 14 kms

Time 3.5 to 4 hours

OS Map Explorer 168

Starting Point Hookshouse Lane, Westonbirt - OS reference 862903

Parking Free on-street parking in Hookshouse Lane

Reaching the start from Bristol Go east on the M4. Leave by Junction 18 and then go north on the A46. After about 5 miles, take the A433 off to the right, signed to Tetbury. Beyond Didmarton pass the entrance to the Westonbirt Arboretum and soon look out for the lane off to the left, just before the Hare and Hounds Hotel

Refreshments Hare and Hounds Hotel, Westonbirt; numerous options in Tetbury; Cat and Custard Pot, Shipton Moyne

THIS GRAND TOUR of the Gloucestershire countryside takes in several country estates, the unique market town of Tetbury and the quintessential Cotswold village of Shipton Moyne. This is a relatively easy walk, the terrain being generally level and the route mainly following easily navigable tracks and footpaths.

The walk starts on the fringes of the Westonbirt Estate, near to the Arboretum, but soon enters the fields of the Elmestree and Highgrove Estates, with distant views of the houses. Beyond here the attractive vista of Tetbury appears on the skyline. The Church of St Mary is built on the site of a Saxon monastery built in 681; there is plenty besides to explore in this historic town. Beyond Tetbury the walk continues through the parkland, paddocks and fields of the Escourt Estate, as it heads towards the village of Shipton Moyne. Beyond here, after passing various farm holdings, you traverse the Westonbirt Estate; passing through its parkland and skirting the former Westonbirt House (now a school) before returning to the starting point.

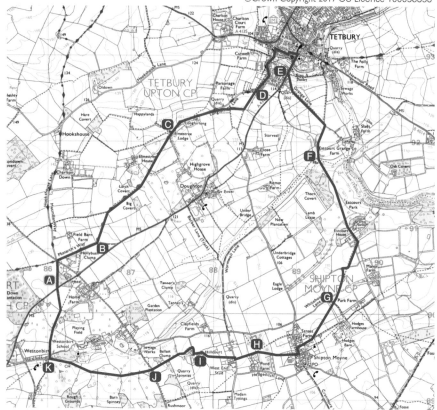

A Walk along Hookshouse Lane, with the hotel on your right to a crossing of various paths and roads. Cross the road joining from the right to a field gate immediately opposite, marked Ashworth Cottage. Go through the gate and proceed along the driveway to the stile ahead. Go over the stile on to a fenced/hedged track. Carry on through three further gates to enter a field. In the field follow the left-hand hedge for 200 metres. Look out for a stile on your left.

B Cross the stile into another field. Bear right and uphill towards a stile in a stone wall about 75 metres from the far right-hand corner of the field. Cross this and head diagonally up the next field to take

a stile in the right-hand corner. Bear right with the path, with the wall/hedge on your right. Pass through a gap in the wall ahead at the field corner. Continue along the hedge and take a stone stile in the corner to enter an open field. Cross a wooden stile in the far boundary. Continue in the same direction, with Elmestree House away to your left and aiming towards the left of the woodland ahead. Cross the tarmac drive. Proceed towards the gate ahead. There may be occasional glimpses of Highgrove, largely hidden in the trees away on the right. Pass through the two field gates in close succession. In the next field, bear left away from Highgrove and in the direction of a metal field gate. Go through

the path alongside. Follow the path over various stiles, through a paddock, and onwards as it narrows into a ginnel adjacent to the back gardens of houses on the right. Eventually you emerge via a wooden stile on to a road. Walk down the road to cross the ford. Climb the subsequent short, steep hill until you reach West Street on your right. Here turn right and proceed until you reach a car park on your left. Bear left through the car park to pick up Old Brewery Lane and continue until you reach the main road opposite St Mary's church. Cross the road, turn right and go steeply downhill. Cross the bridge and after passing the Old Toll House look out for a footpath off to the left.

E Take the stile and proceed up the track, keeping to the right-hand boundary wall. Proceed over a stile and then two others across a driveway. Continue into a field, keeping to the right-hand boundary. Enter a copse to cross three stiles in close succession, again keeping to the right-hand boundary. Exit into a field and towards an avenue of trees. Proceed along the avenue towards double field gates, with an adjacent stone stile. Cross into the next field and immediately turn right, keeping close to the right-hand boundary. Gradually descend to the bottom of the field. Ignore a gate on your right and instead take the stile ahead. After about a further 50 metres, take another gate on the right and go down steps to a stream. Cross a stone bridge and a wooden bridge and then climb a stile to enter parkland via the Palladian Way.

F The route within the parkland is well waymarked. Climb ahead and proceed uphill in a straight line for about 300 metres, looking out for the white posts. When you reach a drive ahead, turn

this and head diagonally right across the next field in the direction of a house in the corner. Go through two successive gates, passing Elmestree Lodge on your left, to enter a lane.

C Follow the lane, as it curves round to the right and passes Longfurlong House. Just beyond the grounds of the house, look out for a stone stile on the right. Take this and turn left to proceed in parallel with the lane. Cross a track via two stiles. Continue ahead to pick up and follow a stream on your left. Eventually you reach a stile in the boundary ahead, leading into woodland. Cross this stile and then immediately go left over a footbridge. After the footbridge, continue ahead through woodland until you reach a stile in the far left-hand corner. Take this and cross the field ahead keeping towards the right-hand boundary. Pass to the left of a bungalow to reach a stile.

D Take the stile and cross the road. Turn right and proceed for about 50 metres until you reach number 18. Here turn left and through a couple of gates to take

right on to it. You now keep with the drive for about 700 metres, as it proceeds to and through gates, towards Estcourt House. Past the gates, continue past outbuildings and a walled garden to reach a cottage on your right. Immediately beyond here take a footpath off to the right. Walk ahead for about 50 metres, between the fence and wall, to take a stile. Bear left for about a further 50 metres towards a gate into a paddock. Enter the paddock and walk half-left looking for a similar gate to exit from on the other side. Go through this gate, climb the stone stile opposite and then turn right towards another similar paddock gate. In the next paddock go half-left towards another similar gate on the far side. Go through this gate and another one immediately opposite. Then go right with a paddock fence on your left to reach a stile.

G Climb this stile, cross the track and immediately climb another stile. Cross the field to take two further stiles in close succession. Cross the next field towards a stile halfway along the left-hand hedgerow, aiming just to the right of the church tower of Shipton Moyne ahead on the horizon. Go over two stiles into the next field and then head right and diagonally towards the wall in the far left-hand corner. Cross the stile and join the walled path ahead into Shipton Moyne. You reach a junction onto the main road. Turn left along the road, crossing to the Cat and Custard Pot Inn. Immediately beyond the pub take the footpath on the right between houses. Take the stile ahead, bear right through two paddocks, crossing two further stiles. In the next field head towards a gap in the trees in the far boundary to reach another stile, adjacent to a field gate.

H Cross the stile and in the next field keep towards the left-hand boundary. Walk ahead through recently planted trees in the direction of houses gradually becoming visible in the distance to a stile in the left-hand corner. Take this stile and now keep to the right-hand boundary to pass through a horse riding area and to cross another stile. Continue through the next field with the right-hand boundary until you reach a stile on to a lane. Take the stile, turn right on the lane and proceed for about 50 metres until you take a stile on your left. In the field, turn sharp left towards and through a field gate. Cross the next field to a stile opposite. In the following field, bear right towards a metal gate just to the right of the farmhouse ahead. Climb the stile next to the gate and then within 20 metres take a further stile off to your left to enter the farm complex.

I Pick up the surfaced driveway in front of the farmhouse and follow this as it meanders through various farm buildings. Just after passing the last set of buildings, look out for a track leading to a field gate on your left. Take the track and go through the gate, keeping to the left-hand boundary. Go through another gate and then keep with the boundary as the track turns left. Within about 50 metres, ignore the gate immediately ahead. Instead turn right, keeping with the left-hand boundary towards another field gate ahead. Go through this and in the next field bear slightly right towards the corner of the woodland. Beyond this corner, go straight ahead across the field to pick up a stile in the hedge ahead.

J Take the stile and cross the road to take another stile and enter the parkland of the Westonbirt estate. Walk ahead to take the stile in the wire fence ahead. Enter the field and follow the right-hand boundary. Take another stile and proceed in parallel with the right-hand boundary, to go through a kissing gate. Continue in the same direction, with Westonbirt School increasingly evident to your right. Go through another kissing gate and over another stile adjacent to a field gate. In the next field bear diagonally right via a further stile and over a track to take a double stile into a golf course. On the golf course turn right in the direction of the clubhouse, avoiding golf balls. Here you pick up the driveway and follow this left in the direction of Westonbirt village. Once you have passed through the gateway of the golf course to reach the public road, look out (within about 50 metres) for a driveway off to the right, marked to Westonbirt School.

K Go up the metalled driveway, with the school eventually reappearing over to the right before you reach a T-junction with the main driveway. Cross the main driveway and immediately enter the open land opposite via a gate. Initially proceed along the boundary on the right but as soon as you see a gate ahead bear left to take it. From the gate, look out carefully for an indistinct footpath bearing off to the left. Bear left towards a telegraph pole ahead. Upon reaching the telegraph pole, bear further left towards the main road and a visible sign for the Hare and Hounds Hotel. Eventually a stile in a stone wall becomes apparent ahead, to the left of the sign. Take this stile and then cross the main road at its junction with Hookshouse Lane, where the walk started. **A**

North Nibley, Stinchcombe Hill and Coombe Hill

Distance 10 miles / 16 kms

Time 5.5 hours

OS Map Explorer 167

Starting Point St Martin's Church, The Street, North Nibley - OS reference 736962

Parking Plenty of free on-road parking along The Street, especially by the church

Reaching the start from Bristol Go north on the M5. Leave by Junction 14. Go north up the A38 via Stone and continue through Newport. At Heathfield take the second right turn on to the lane signed for North Nibley. Follow the signs to reach the church at the near edge of the village

Refreshments Black Horse, North Nibley or New Inn, Waterley Bottom; numerous seats on the circuit for picnics

---

THIS WEST COTSWOLD walk explores beautiful wooded escarpments, the high open plateau of Stinchcombe Hill and undulating farmland in the vicinity of Waterley Bottom. There are spectacular panoramic views, especially from Drakestone Point, Heartbreak Hill and the Tyndale Tower. Although much of the terrain is flat, there are two long steep climbs and one long steep descent, making it a demanding walk. Most of the route is on well-defined tracks and footpaths, more than half along the Cotswold Way.

From the start, at the attractive village of North Nibley, you soon climb the wooded slopes up to the golf course on Stinchcombe Hill. As the views open out, you do an almost complete circuit of the plateau before exiting into woodland on the slopes above Dursley. There follows a steep descent down Heartbreak Hill into Waterley Bottom. From here the route climbs again in the direction of Wotton-under-Edge. You eventually reach Coombe Hill where there are further views. You continue along the escarpment above Wotton and then follow the western Cotswold escarpment, passing through Westridge Wood and skirting an Iron-Age fort before emerging on Nibley Knoll. After the opportunity to climb the Tyndale Monument, the route curves back downhill to North Nibley and the starting point.

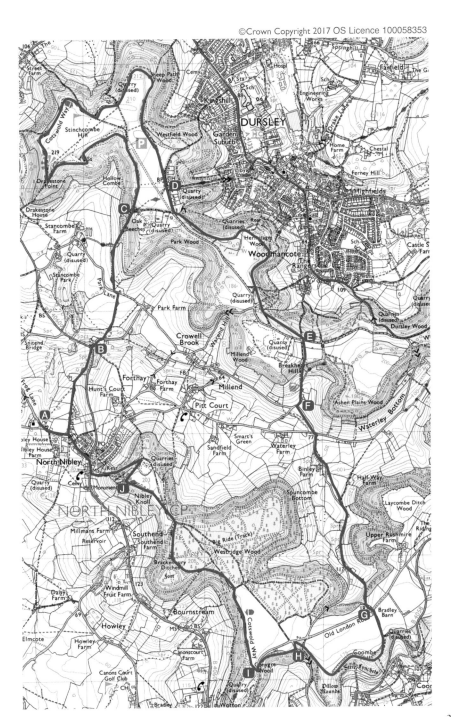

29

A From the church travel along The Street towards the village centre for about 200 metres. On reaching the triangular island at the top of Lower House Lane, take the marked Cotswold Way down the lane, with the playing field over to your left. At the end of the cul-de-sac continue down the narrow hedged footpath. There are attractive views ahead and to either side. You keep on downhill. The path broadens and passes through woodland before eventually reaching a busy road. Cross the road and go down the minor road immediately opposite. Pass three houses on the left. As the lane curves round to the right you pass a further house on the right.

B Just beyond this house, take a footpath through a gap in a hedge. Go up through a gate into a field. Go up the field to the marked waymark post and then curve left further uphill and through a gate. Continue on up the next field past a waymark towards a house at the foot of the hill. Take a gate on to a road. Turn left and within about 50 metres go up steps to take a gate off to the right. Go straight up the field and through a gate in the fence. In the next field turn left alongside the fence. Continue in the same direction along the whole field, with wooded slopes up to your right. Go through a gate to enter the woodland ahead. Take a wooden bridge, which crosses a track below, to reach a junction with a wide track. Turn right up the wide track. Continue on uphill as the track becomes steeper. At a crossroads of tracks, keep straight-ahead. As you near the top of the hill, take the right-hand fork. Continue uphill, cross a further track and exit the woodland on to a golf course.

C Turn left along the path abutting the woodland on your left and the golf course on your right. Keep with this path. As you climb gradually, spectacular views open up on the left. There are plenty of seats at which you can stop to enjoy them. Keep with the path as it reaches the plateau of Stinchcombe Hill. The path curves left around the escarpment as the spectacular views continue. For a long stretch there is no need to deviate down on to any parallel paths running along the hillside or into the adjacent woodland. For this section through to Drakestone Point you simply stick closely within the boundary edge of the golf course, following the waymarks.

Bear right at a junction of paths, to remain within the golf course and alongside the woodland. When you reach a T-junction turn right and soon afterwards take the right-hand fork uphill through scrubland. You keep with the edge of the golf course, all the way until you reach Drakestone Point. From Drakestone Point keep on with the boundary path, soon passing Stinchcombe Hill trig point. The path descends slightly towards a stone-built viewing shelter on your left. Pass this and keep ahead into woodland. However, you very soon turn right twice to exit the woodland back on to the edge of the golf course. From here, continue with the Cotswold Way signs as you further circuit the plateau of Stinchcombe Hill and the golf course, with woodland still to your left. Follow the path in and (mainly) out the woodland; always sticking near and at a similar level to the golf course. Keep within the golf course wherever the waymarks allow you. Eventually you pass Stinchcombe Hill House on your left. Just beyond here keep straight ahead at the crossroads of paths. Stay near the edge of the golf course and follow waymarks in and out of the woodland (in places there may be more than one 'right' option, but do remember to keep the golf course within your sights). When the clubhouse appears on the horizon, follow the clearly defined path cutting across the golf course towards it.

D Pass immediately in front of the clubhouse. At a waymark post continue ahead, taking the path along the left-hand boundary with houses to reach the lane leading into the driveway of the golf club. Very briefly join this lane before taking another lane down to the left, signed to Dursley. Go down this lane for less than 100 metres. Take a broad track off to the right into woodland. Immedi-

ately take the uphill right-hand fork. Continue along the track through woodland following the blue and red arrow signs on the trees when you can, being careful not to stray far downhill. Continue over a crossing track and ahead with the waymarks on the trees. Take the first clear turn off to the right following the inner edge of the woodland, with a field over to your right. Carry on straight ahead until a further track merges in from the left. Soon the track curves sharply right following the edge of the escarpment. Keep uphill on the track. When a green barrier (leading on to a road) appears about 100 metres ahead, immediately look out for a junction with two tracks turning off to the left. Take the straighter and lesser of these two turns. Follow the path through the woodland for about 100 metres in parallel with the audible/visible road over to your right. Do not continue ahead when you reach a crossing track. Instead turn left on this track for about 50 metres and then take a further track off to the right. Continue downhill on this track for about 100 metres and then take the right-hand fork. You now stick closely with the same (sometimes muddy) track as it undulates and curves around the hillside. Ignoring any lesser adjoining paths, continue with this main track until reaching a definite T-junction with another main track joining from the left. Here turn right and go uphill through the woodland to emerge out on to the road.

E Cross the road and take the track immediately opposite, adjacent to a fire hydrant marked 610. Follow the wooded track down towards the edge of the hill. As the track sweeps round to the right, you continue straight ahead on a path steeply down woodland on the side of Breakheart Hill. Cross a stile and go down through scrub into a field. Go straight downhill initially in the direction of a distant road sign that you will shortly pass, and gradually close in on the left-hand boundary. As the New Inn appears over to your left, join the left-hand boundary and follow it down. Go through a gate down (a sometimes slippery) slope on to a lane opposite the New Inn. Continue down the road to a junction.

F Keep ahead along the lane signed to Wotton-under-Edge. Cross a further road junction and again take the Wotton road straight ahead. This section is a very narrow enclosed lane with steep banks but you will not need to walk too far on it. Very soon follow a sign to take the wooded footpath along the top of the left-hand bank. Carry on ahead on this path for about 200 metres until you cross a stile into a field. Turn right and continue with the right-hand boundary of this long field. Eventually you exit via a stile at the corner to return to the lane. Carry on along the (now wider) lane until you reach Apple Tree Farm on the right. Immediately opposite the farm buildings take an easily missed ancient track turning off to the left. This enclosed green lane continues steeply uphill, initially passing through fields and then through woodland. Tracks join from both the left and right, before you eventually emerge via Laycombe Wood, managed by the Woodland Trust, to a road at the top.

G Cross the road. Walk straight ahead on the level along a hedged/walled path. When the path curves away to the left and downhill, go through a gate ahead into a field. Take the right-hand path, which follows the boundary wall just below the summit of Coombe Hill, with the village of Coombe below to your left. The path follows round the head of the

coombe. Stay with the right-hand boundary all the way, including when you reach a corner. This takes you uphill through a gate and on to a track. Enter woodland and continue gently uphill on the track. Keep on ahead. As the track curves round to the right and as you near the road (you can hear the traffic and if you can see a field gate ahead you may have come too far) keep straight ahead on a lesser path. Continue on this for about 100 metres until going through a gate to reach the road junction. Turn left downhill on the lane for less than 100 metres.

H Take a gate up to the right to enter Conygre Wood. Continue on the path with the contours. You pass buildings and a play area up to the right. Continue until you reach an information board on your left opposite to an obvious parking area up to the right. Here take the right-hand turn uphill out of the woodland. Cross the road and go left for 50 metres. Beyond the parking area, take the right-hand turn. Follow the hedged track uphill towards woodland to reconnect with the Cotswold Way.

I Turn right along the well waymarked Cotswold Way route, which soon enters Westridge Wood. Follow along the edge of the woodland adjacent to a long field over to the right. Where the path divides bear left to take the central of the three options. Keep ahead through the woodland on the well-surfaced path, which gradually climbs uphill. Bear right with the Cotswold Way waymark at the next junction and soon afterwards bear right again. You soon skirt Brackenbury Ditches, an Iron-Age hill fort. Immediately past here turn right at a junction of paths and continue downhill. A track merges in from the left before you reach an obvious major junction of several paths. At the waymark post turn left and

then through a gate. Continue on the track and shortly exit the woodland into open land. You immediately see the Tyndale Monument ahead. Follow the left-hand boundary up the large field to reach the monument, built in 1866 in honour of William Tyndale, English translator of the Bible, who was born in North Nibley. It is well worth climbing to the top if you can – on a clear day the Severn Estuary and the Welsh hills are clearly visible.

J With the monument immediately behind you, follow the left-hand edge of the field for 150 metres. Follow a waymark post directing you left and downhill. Take the narrow path into woodland past the remnants of a stile. Continue downhill on this path until a T-junction with a crossing track. Here turn left and keep steeply downhill on the broad track all the way down to the main road. You are now back in North Nibley. Cross the road and turn right. You soon reach the Black Horse public house, over to the right. Turn left to take The Street and return in the direction of the church. **A**

No. 6

Saltford, Kelston and Newbridge

Distance 9 miles / 14.5 kms

Time 4 to 4.5 hours

OS Map Explorer 155

Starting Point The old railway bridge, High Street, Saltford - OS reference 687675

Parking Free parking in small lay-by just beyond the old railway bridge or nearby

Reaching the start from Bristol Go out of Bristol on the A4 Bath Road to Saltford. Turn left into Beech Road and then right into the High Street. Carry on downhill past the Bird in Hand public house on the right and under the bridge

Refreshments Bird in Hand, Saltford; The Old Crown Inn, Kelston; The Boathouse, Newbridge. There is also a picnic seat with panoramic views at Prospect Stile

---

THIS WALK explores the countryside of the Avon Valley between Saltford and Bath, including the hills of the southern Cotswolds. It incorporates splendid panoramic views, attractive riverside scenery and the villages of Kelston and North Stoke. The walking is mainly on tracks and footpaths, including a peaceful riverside stretch and the Bristol and Bath Railway cycle path. There are couple of stretching climbs but the terrain is mostly flat.

The walk starts besides the old railway bridge at Saltford. After a brief introduction to the cycle path the route passes across fields to Kelston village. From here there is a sustained climb up the slopes of Kelston Round Hill until the track levels out and curves round the hillside. As the track contours the hillside, there are excellent views down to the valley below. Passing through North Stoke village, the route then climbs steeply past Bath racecourse and towards Prospect Stile and the best panoramic views of the walk. There follows a leisurely descent towards and around the eastern edge of Kelston Round Hill and skirting the edge of the built up area of Bath. The route eventually descends down through Oldfield to the River Avon at Newbridge. After crossing the river you stick closely to the riverside before reaching the cycle path bridge. The final stretch is straight along the wooded cycle path with glimpses of the river below.

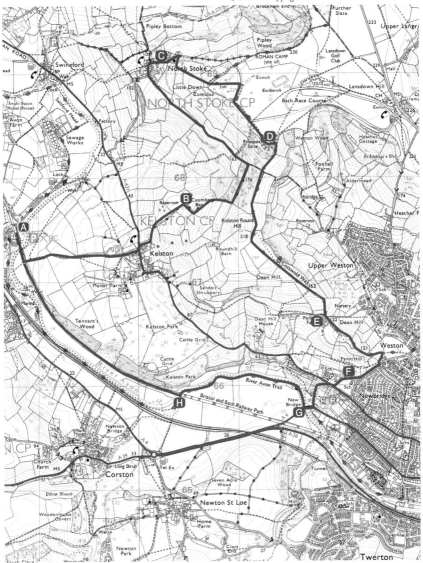

A From the lay-by follow the inclined path up to the cycle path but do not join the main path. Instead keep to the left, following the narrow, enclosed footpath, which runs in parallel across the bridge. Carry on for about 100 metres until you reach concrete steps down to the left, before a further bridge. Descend these steps and go through a metal gate on to a track. Turn left and uphill along the fenced track. Go through a field gate. In the next field, keep to the right-hand boundary and go through another field gate. Go straight ahead through a further field gate and then immediately take a small gate off to its right to enter the

fenced field. Proceed with the track to your left and in the direction of barns ahead. Go through the field gate in the left-hand corner of the field and then immediately take the gate ahead into the next field. Continue on the raised path between trees, with the barns now immediately on your left. Go through another gate. Carry on ahead and through a further gate in the left-hand corner. You then immediately turn left on the crossing track and go through a further gate. Now go diagonally over two crossing drives and through the metal gate ahead. Now follow the narrow hedged path; this soon morphs into a lane leading to the main road of Kelston. The Old Crown Inn is off to the right. Turn left on the road for 50 metres. Cross to take the lane opposite. Follow this lane steeply uphill as it goes left and right for about 400 metres. Continue with it as it bends right and passes in front of Coombe Barn, which has been converted into holiday cottages.

B From Coombe Barn continue with the lane as it proceeds uphill, now more as a track, to a sharp left-hand bend.

Continue with the track as it ascends more steeply to reach a further left-hand bend. Continue round left with the wooded track and then keep straight along the hillside for about a further 300 metres and through a gate to a T-junction of tracks. Turn left and initially go downhill. Go through a gate to pick up a fenced path. Follow this level path all the way to the village of North Stoke, as it contours the hillside and curves right, with fine views off to the left. Eventually you descend to a junction with the road in North Stoke. Here go straight ahead with the road to pass through the village. Continue with the road as it curves to the right. Pass a letter box on the left and continue uphill towards the church.

C As the road peters out in front of the church, continue with the metalled track that curves to the left. After about 50 metres enter a metal field gate off to the right into a small field, along a track leading parallel to the edge of the churchyard. Take a stile in the left-hand corner by a further metal gate to enter a large field. In the field, keep to the right-hand boundary for about 200 metres.

Keep with the churchyard boundary again initially, until you reach a waymark post. Follow the waymark directions by bearing left up the field to take a visible stile in the fence. In the next field proceed more steeply uphill to a waymark post visible ahead on the skyline. At this post initially bear right up the distinct track but after about 50 metres curve left towards a field gate up on the horizon. Continue uphill on the track, proceeding past a copse on your left, to reach the metal gate at the top. Pass through the gate and continue on the, soon level, track across a field. Enter the next field, immediately cross a ditch and follow the track around to the right. Keep the ditch and the field boundary to your right. At the corner of the field continue left, with the field boundary still on your right until you reach the bounds of Bath racecourse. Go through a gate into the racecourse, keeping the boundary to your right until you reach Prospect Stile (actually a gate) in the right-hand corner. The views from here are spectacular on a fine day.

D Go through the gate, descend past a seat and through a copse. Shortly pass through another gate and then continue to descend. For a considerable distance from here you can simply stick with the Cotswold Way signs. Follow the waymarks downhill and through a high gate on to a crossing path. Here go immediately left through another gate and then immediately right through a further gate. Proceed on the level fenced path to approach and skirt the perimeter of Kelston Round Hill, going through a gate en route. (You soon reach an obvious right-hand turn detouring to the top of Kelston Round Hill, if you prefer. You can then either descend back to it or alternatively re-join the same footpath about 600 metres further along.) The main route continues on the same path, soon passing the return junction for the optional detour (a gate off to the right). From here continue on the same fenced/hedged path for at least a further 1000 metres. With Bath becoming increasingly evident down to your left, you eventually descend to reach a tarmac lane.

E Continue on the lane for about 20 metres. Take the stile immediately ahead, still signed for the Cotswold Way, to enter a field. Contour the field, gradually climbing towards the top right-hand corner, where you are guided via a gate into a hedged track. Soon a trig point appears just off to the right, from which there are panoramic views. Continue on down the track and through a gate to enter another field. Descend steeply down the centre of the field and through another gate into a recreation ground. Here turn right along a hedge to exit via a narrow gap on to a road. Cross the road and turn right. Pass Franklands Close on the left and continue for about 250 metres. As the road starts to bends

round to the left, cross it again via the pedestrian refuge.

F Immediately take a slip-road leading to a track between houses, scrubland and school grounds. When the track reaches Kelston Road, cross the road and turn right for about 50 metres, looking out for a footpath opposite the main entrance to Oldfield School. Go down the steps and through the gate. Follow the path down steps through a copse. At the bottom enter a meadow. Keep to the left-hand hedge before reaching a junction with another footpath. Here turn right and continue ahead, crossing the driveway serving a boathouse. Continue ahead, passing between the park and ride on the left and The Boathouse pub, which becomes visible ahead on the right. Keep to the left of The Boathouse and go through the car park to take the steps ahead up to the road bridge. At the top, turn right to cross the bridge and then take the path on the right to descend to the opposite bank of the River Avon.

G You now keep with the footpath immediately next to the river on your right for the next 1500 metres or so. Very shortly you pass through a small copse adjacent to a waterworks. However, you soon emerge once more into open countryside. Eventually you reach a bridge carrying the old railway, now the cycle path you briefly walked alongside at the beginning of the walk, over the river.

H Take the steps up the embankment before the bridge to connect with the cycle path. Turn right and simply follow the cycle path for about 2000 metres. Beware of cyclists as it can be very busy. Continue until you reach the bridge re-crossing the river. At the end of the bridge, there is a left-hand turn down to the Bird in Hand. Immediately opposite to this, on the right-hand side of the cycle path is the path you climbed at the start of the walk. This leads you back down to the layby where you started. **A**

Backwell and Barrow Court

Distance 9 miles / 14.5 kms

Time 4.5 to 5 hours

OS Map Explorer 154

Starting Point St Andrew's Church, Church Lane, Backwell - OS reference 493683

Parking Plenty of free on-road parking near to the church

Reaching the start from Bristol Take the A370 out of Bristol. Continue through Flax Bourton to reach the village of Backwell. As you enter the village pass The George public house on the right and then look out for Church Lane off to the left. Follow this along until you reach the church

Refreshments None on route but a short diversion towards the end of the walk to The Rising Sun. Also other options in Backwell

---

THIS WALK explores the diverse woodland and undulating farmland to the south of Backwell and Flax Bourton. Although it is relatively near to Bristol, skirts several quarry workings and passes within earshot of Bristol Airport it is still rural in character. You traverse the pretty Bourton Combe, pass the historic Barrow Court and enjoy interesting panoramic views. The terrain is undulating but there is only one long climb; this following soon after the long descent through Bourton Combe. The route follows mainly waymarked tracks and footpaths and is likely to be muddy in winter.

The walk climbs out of Backwell via a former quarry now transformed into a local nature reserve. You circumnavigate current and prospective quarry workings before the descent down the wooded Bourton Combe. The route skirts Flax Bourton before climbing past the mainly 16th-century Barrow Court. Beyond here the views open up of the rolling countryside to the north and the city of Bristol over to the east. You skirt a variety of deciduous and coniferous woodland. You then follow an ancient track, Tinker's Lane, which emerges at Oatfield where there are views across to Bristol Airport. The route continues along the wooded escarpment of Healls Scars before emerging on to Long Lane. You descend Long Lane and then curve back down towards Backwell, through further woodland. The final leg is on flat terrain along the edge of Backwell, with the church spire visible some distance ahead before you return to the start.

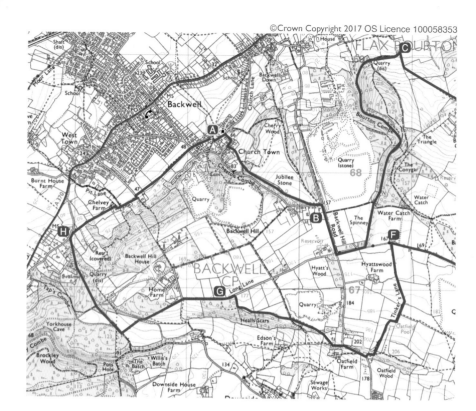

A From the church turn off Church Lane and up Church Town, the lane immediately opposite. Keep with the lane as it curves up to the right past houses. After the fourth house you reach a footpath sign in front of Church Cottage. Turn left to take the metalled driveway uphill between the houses. This soon morphs into a narrow treed footpath. Continue steeply uphill. Go through a gate to enter the Jubilee Stone Wood Nature Reserve. Follow the path uphill through the woodland. Ignore a stile off to the left and pass through an open area. Carry on further up the hill where there is a further open area, with views and the Jubilee Stone over to the left. From here continue ahead with the left-hand fence, within the edge of the woodland. As you approach houses and a field gate ahead, take a stile off to the left to exit the reserve into a field. Bear right across the field and take a gate in the right-hand corner on to a road. Cross the road and take the gate opposite.

B The footpaths in this locality have been affected by quarry workings, resulting in a detour at this point. Turn right on the track, which runs parallel with the road. Continue along the hedged boundary all the way up to the field corner. At the corner continue with the track, now alongside another road, and head towards woodland. On reaching the next corner, continue left with the track alongside the woodland. Go through a gate to enter the woodland to the left of a derelict building. Go ahead on the downhill track. Keep on this track, as it goes deeper into the woodland and be sure to stay with it as it

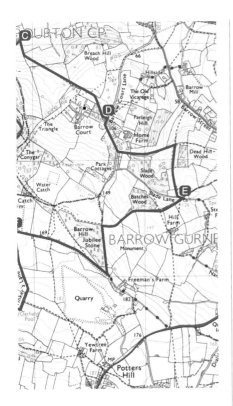

another in the top left-hand corner. Carry on in a similar direction along the middle of the next field, passing in front of Barrow Court. After passing the buildings, bear right to follow the right-hand boundary, adjacent to woodland, in the direction of the driveway. Exit over a stile on to the driveway. (If you wish to make the short diversion to visit Barrow Court church turn right on the driveway and then return to the same point.)

D To continue on the main route, turn left on the driveway and continue ahead to reach a lane. Turn right on the lane. Proceed up the lane for about 200 metres. Just beyond the main entrance to Home Farm, take a footpath via a stile off to the left. Proceed through trees alongside the right-hand boundary to cross a stile and enter a long field. Go down the long field. Initially keep towards the woodland over to the right then, as you reach the bottom, close in on the right-hand boundary fence. In the right-hand corner of the field turn right through a gate. Now climb up the centre of the field towards a stile in the hedgerow. Take the stile and proceed in a straight line through two further fields via stiles. At the end of the narrow third field take a stile to reach a lane.

E Turn left on the lane for about 50 metres. Here go through a gate on to a treed green lane. Carry on up the lane. Exit via a gate to enter a field. Proceed with the right-hand boundary of the field, with woodland soon appearing on your immediate right. Go through a gate on to a fenced/ hedged track. Keep with the track as it climbs gently towards woodland ahead. When you reach the corner of the woodland you also reach a crossing track. Take the left turn and go uphill on this hedged track, with the coniferous woodland over to your right.

curves left further down into Bourton Combe. Towards the bottom the track curves round to the right. At the very bottom the track divides; be sure to take the right-hand fork and follow it back uphill. Soon the track exits the woodland. It then continues downhill as a wooded track until exiting on to the end of a lane, opposite to Combe Cottages. Cross the lane and go through a gate next to the cottages into a field.

C Go uphill with the right-hand hedge and through a gate into another field. Here bear slightly left and uphill to pass through the tall metal gate in the fenced boundary ahead. Keep ahead up the next field aiming just to the left of Barrow Court, now visible on the horizon. You eventually pick up the left-hand boundary of the field and pass a stile before taking

Go through a gate at the end of the woodland to enter a field. Continue up the field to a T-junction of tracks. Turn right and continue downhill with the track eventually curving left and away from the woodland towards the left-hand corner of the field (there are actually two roughly parallel tracks which eventually converge in this corner). Here go through a gate to take a wooded track. Continue ahead on the track. After passing Water Catch Farm, over to your right in the distance, continue for about a further 100 metres to reach a track off to your left.

F Take Tinker's Lane, an ancient track. Continue on this narrow hedged track for about 1000 metres as it wends gently uphill, passing newly planted woodland associated with the quarry workings over to the left. After passing a telephone mast, the track descends to exit on to a driveway. Turn right down the metalled driveway to reach a road. Turn right up the road and continue uphill and past Oatfield Farm, which is down to the left. Distant views of Bristol Airport soon appear in the same direction. As the road bends round to the right in front of a large house, The Grove, take a gate down to the left. Go ahead on the narrow fenced footpath along the top of an embankment. Circumnavigate the outer perimeter of The Grove as far as you can until the path climbs into woodland. Keep up ahead in the woodland towards the fence at the top of the bank. Here bear left with the footpath along the fence, which follows the edge of a further quarry. Continue along the fence until you cross a stile and another track. Go across the chain gate ahead into a field. Keep ahead on the track and then curve to the right with it to reach an open plateau. Now turn left and follow the left-hand field boundary adjacent to woodland. In the left-hand corner take the gap ahead into the woodland. Keep on the path within the inner edge of the woodland until exiting via a stile into a field. Carry on in the same direction within the field, keeping within about 10 metres of the outer edge of the woodland. In the far left-hand corner of the field, take a stile to re-enter the woodland. Immediately turn right and keep with the path which runs near to the right-hand boundary. Curve round left with the woodland alongside a lane that appears ahead. Eventually you reach a signed exit, over a metal bar, on to the lane.

G Turn left on the tarmac lane. You stay on this lane, proceeding gently downhill for about 1000 metres. You have further views towards the airport over to the left before passing the junction to Home Farm over to the right. Continue downhill past Magpie Hill as the lane becomes more of a wooded track. Ignore the crossing Avon Cycleway Link and continue until you reach a T-junction. Here you turn right. Keep ahead on the track adjacent to woodland on the left and a field over to the right, at the end of which the

track enters woodland. Keep ahead gently uphill, go over a crossing track and continue until the track merges with a metalled drive. Now descend the drive quite steeply through woodland to exit out on to a lane.

H Turn right down the lane. Within about 50 metres take a stile into a field next to a gate marked as Bristol Waterworks. Follow the track uphill with the left-hand boundary of the field and through a gap into another field. Continue ahead in the same direction and over a stile. Carry on along the next field, taking your bearing on the now visible Backwell church and closing in on the left-hand boundary towards Chelvey Farm, more immediately ahead. Take a gate in the left-hand corner to divert round Chelvey Farm. Follow the fenced path to pick up a lane in front of the property. (After 50 metres you could divert to the Rising Sun in Backwell by taking the track down to the left.) However, to continue on the main route, keep down the lane until it bends sharply left. Here take the gate off to the right. Take a path running alongside the right-hand wall. Carry on straight-ahead through three fields, initially keeping towards the right-hand boundary. Passing through various gates on route, stick to a course just to the left of the church tower ahead. As you reach the built-up area again, go through a gate on to Church Town. Cross the road and turn left down to the junction with Church Lane. Cross and turn right up Church Lane. Pass the primary school on the right and follow the lane up as it curves round to reach the church and your starting point. **A**

Castle Combe, North Wraxall and Ford

Distance 10 miles / 16 kms

Time 5 to 5.5 hours

OS Map Explorer 156

Starting Point Car park off B4039, Castle Combe - OS reference 845777

Parking Free long-stay car park

Reaching the start from Bristol Go east on the M4. Leave by Junction 18 and then go north on the A46. After about two miles, at Old Sodbury take the B4040 off to the right, signed to Acton Turville and Castle Combe. Upon reaching Acton Turville, bear right to pick up the B4039. Continue on through Burton to reach the edge of Castle Combe. Turn off to the right, following the sign into the car park

Refreshments Castle Inn Hotel or White Hart, Castle Combe or White Hart, Ford

---

THIS WALK explores the wooded combes, streams, meadows and stone villages at the southern tip of the Cotswolds. The terrain is undulating, with a couple of steep climbs. The route is mainly on tracks and well-defined paths. There are couple of muddy stretches.

It starts with a descent into and through the picturesque village of Castle Combe, centred on the old market cross. You continue on through the Castle Combe golf course and Manor estate and along the Broadmead valley to West Kington. From here the route crosses mainly flat terrain towards North Wraxall. From North Wraxall there is a descent into Doncombe Bottom, after which there is a steep climb through woodland to reach Colerne Down, followed by a scenic descent towards the river valley below. Once you reach the By Brook valley you follow this as far as Ford after which there is a steep ascent. The walk proceeds on through meadows and woodland and the village of Long Dean, before finally ascending and descending through further woodland back to Castle Combe.

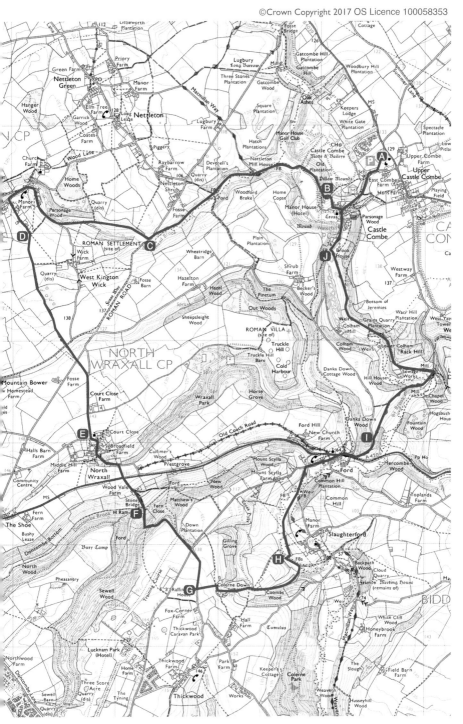

A Leave the car park by way of steps and turn right downhill on the lane. In about 50 metres turn right again going downhill to the Market Cross in the centre of Castle Combe. Bear right around the front of the Castle Inn Hotel and through the underpass beneath the house ahead. Proceed along the private road until it becomes a walled path. Stay with the path as it climbs and goes beneath a small bridge. Almost immediately after the bridge the path climbs up to a gate in a wall.

B Go through the gate to enter woodland. Turn left and follow the path as it descends alongside the wall on your left, emerging from the woodland with a view of the Manor Golf Course ahead. Follow the clearly defined path ahead down to a stone bridge. Bear left to cross this. Follow the surfaced path for about 150 metres until, immediately before this crosses a river, you see a clear footpath sign directing you off left into woodland. Once in the woodland, follow the path through the trees alongside the river on your right until you pass through a wrought iron gate indicating the end of the Manor grounds. Go towards the houses on your left converted from what was once a mill. Turn left to take the track passing between the two houses. Follow the path from here through a gate and woodland, with the river now on your left, for about 200 metres until you reach an old stone packhorse bridge by a ford. Do not cross the bridge but instead go through a small gate ahead of it on the right-hand side. Immediately climb right up the bank into woodland. Proceed in the same direction as before, in parallel with the river, now below. Exit the woodland via a gate and continue through a further gate and through open land fenced to the right. Re-enter woodland, within which the path is often muddy. The path wends up and down within sight of the river and eventually emerges out on to a lane by way of a further gate. Turn left on this lane and proceed downhill for less than 100 metres.

C Go through a field gate ahead of you on the right to enter a field. You continue along the valley in parallel with the river. Keep to the main track, which soon bears left to run along a river embankment, about 50 metres above the river. Ignore all turns off to the right up the hillside. Continue ahead through a gate at the end of the long field. Bear left closer towards the river's edge and shortly cross by a way of a stone bridge. With the river now on your right, carry on up the track through the trees until it emerges on to a lane. Here turn right and proceed with the lane as it curves around to the left to reach the centre of the village of West Kington. Do not cross the bridge over to your right. Instead turn left on the road signed to Marshfield. Climb the road for about 200 metres until you reach a sharp left hand turn, leading uphill. Climb this lane to soon reach Pound Cottage and other buildings associated with Manor Farm. Continue ahead on the lane for a further 200 metres until on your left you reach Woodbine Cottage.

D You are now at the junction of several footpaths. Turn right to continue along the same lane, as the tarmac surface abruptly ceases and it becomes more of a track. The lane continues between typical Cotswold limestone walls for about another 500 metres, passing through the edge of woodland before reaching an open field with the hedge/wall on the left only. Continue through this and into the next field, where you soon pass through a wide gap in the left-hand wall into the adjoining field. Continue with

the path in a similar direction with the wall now on your right-hand side until you reach a lane. Cross this and climb over the stile ahead. In the next field, which drops into a hollow, proceed down and up on the line of a telegraph pole to a gate. Then take the left boundary of the next field to exit via a field gate on to a lane. Cross the lane and then climb a stile immediately opposite. Go ahead across the field just to the right of the electricity pylon towards a visible stile. This stile leads out on to a further lane. Turn right on this towards North Wraxall continuing for about 500 metres until you reach the church on your left.

E At the road junction next to the church, turn left. Drop down the hill through the village and start to climb the hill until just before you reach Southwood Cottage on your left. Here take the waymarked path off to the right. Proceed ahead up the wooded path in the direction of the audible A420 road. Cross the road straight over to the metalled track opposite and proceed gradually downhill in the same direction for 150 metres towards a bungalow on the left. Here take the right-hand (not the left-hand) of the two paths immediately ahead of you. The path drops down steeply into woodland. It then proceeds along a fenced strip between two fields before you cross a wooden bridge into a larger area of woodland.

F Bear right with the normally muddy path and climb steeply upwards through the woods for about 100 metres until you reach a major junction of paths. Here go ahead for a further 20 metres and up steps to reach a further crossing track. Turn left to take this track, which continues to climb but more gradually and then swings round to the right. Continue on, with a distinct valley now

down to your left, until the point at which the track begins to curve away to the left. Here take a footpath ahead leading out of the woodland. After no more than 10 metres you reach a gap in the wall at the boundary of the woodland. Exit the woodland into a field. Turn left and follow the woodland boundary to and through a field gate on to a main road. Cross this road to a lane signposted to Euridge. Follow this for about 250 metres until you reach a driveway on your left.

G Go through the gate and follow this track. Proceed downhill on the gravel track, winding right and left and passing through Colerne Down Farm. Go over a stile and about 100 metres downhill beyond the farm, look out for a right-hand fork in the tracks. Take this and proceed towards the edge of the woodland ahead. Bear left with the woodland edge (keeping out of the woodland). Follow the grassy track downhill, with the woodland as your right-hand boundary. The village of Slaughterford increasingly comes into view as you progress further downhill. At the bottom of the field go over a stile and proceed immediately ahead to the river. Go left along the river for about 100 metres.

H On reaching a metal footbridge, cross the weir and turn left. Bear right along the river meadow towards a stile ahead in the corner. Cross the stile and bear slightly right again, proceeding to cross another stile in the corner. In the next field go straight ahead towards a footbridge. Cross the footbridge and in the following field keep with the riverbank in the direction of the houses ahead, to take a stile onto a lane. Turn right along the lane, past the White Hart Inn and through Ford to reach the A420. Cross the A420 to the bus shelter. Turn right and proceed for about 100 metres towards the lane off to the left at the side of Bybrook Barn. Take this lane and

proceed steeply uphill for about 200 metres until you reach a footpath.

I Take a stile on your right and proceed on the visible contoured path for about 100 metres before crossing a further stile on to a track. Turn right along this fenced track to enter woodland and then reach a field gate. Go through this and proceed downhill with what is initially a walled and subsequently a sunken track. When you reach the village of Long Dean proceed straight-ahead in the same direction, ignoring various footpaths left and right. Eventually you reach a road junction, with a letter box immediately ahead. Here take the lane/track to the left, passing Rose Cottage on your right and then a converted mill on your left. Climb uphill, ignoring the sewage works off to the left, as the track enters woodland and swings round towards two sets of field gates ahead. Go over the stiles adjacent to each of these. Carry on with the track through woodland and as the

river valley opens out below, for a short while. Keep to the path as it re-enters woodland, sticking to the left hand boundary and gradually descending. Keep on downhill, continuing to stick closely to the left-hand boundary, until reaching a gate at the bottom next to the river. Continue with the river to your left for about 50 metres.

J You reach a stone bridge, which you cross to reach the road. You have now returned to Castle Combe. Turn right and continue with the river on your right back to the Market Cross. From here re-trace your steps up to the car park where you started. **A**

Stanton Prior and Priston

Distance 6.5 miles / 10 kms

Time 3 to 3.5 hours

OS Map Explorer 155 and 142

Starting Point St Lawrence Church, Stanton Prior - OS reference 677627

Parking Free on-road parking near to the church

Reaching the start from Bristol Head out toward Bath on the A4. Go through Saltford. At the Globe Inn roundabout, take the A39 through Corston, then look out for a series of lanes off to the left signed to Stanton Prior – all are narrow but the third lane, just as you reach the edge of Marksbury, is the easiest to navigate

Refreshments Ring O'Bells, Priston

THIS WALK explores the rolling hills, hidden valleys, pleasant farmland and the old villages of Stanton Prior and Priston, to the west of Bath. The walk undulates and includes several climbs but is not difficult. The walking is mainly on tracks and field paths. There is a muddy stretch right at the beginning.

The walk starts in Stanton Prior, one of the oldest recorded villages in the old county of Somerset. You exit the village on a field track which soon morphs into a green lane. You then pick up a path which gradually descends to cross the Conygre valley and then gradually climbs again to skirt Priest Barrow and Farmborough Common. The route then briefly descends again to follow the attractive Newton valley all the way to Priston village. The route passes through the village and then through fields towards Priston Mill, which dates back more than 1000 years, being mentioned in the Domesday Book. Beyond Priston Mill you pick up the Conygre valley again. The route then curves back in the direction of Stanton Prior by means of a steady and steep uphill climb, followed by a descent down an ancient green lane. The final descent back towards the village is via fields and the churchyard of the 12th-century church.

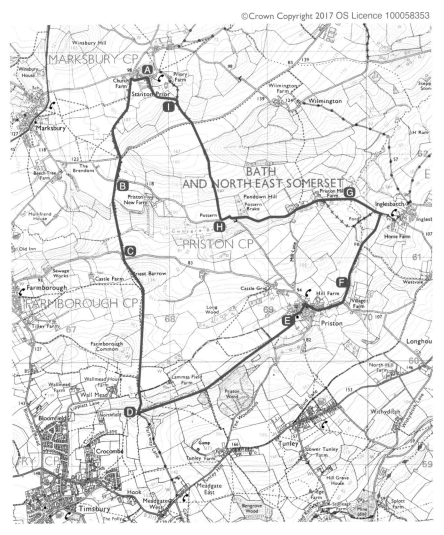

A With the church on your left walk along the road for about 150 metres until it bends to the right. Take the gate off to the left. Follow the muddy track, keeping near to the right-hand boundary, to go through another gate. Enter a hedged green lane and proceed gradually uphill to cross a road. Continue straight ahead on the same green lane. As the terrain flattens out and begins to gently descend, continue until you reach a second road.

B At the second road proceed right for about 30 metres. Take the second of the neighbouring field gates to enter a field. In the field keep to the left hand hedge for about 150 metres until, well before the end of the field, you go left through

a gate in the hedge. In the next field go diagonally right and downhill to go through a further gate. From here follow the left-hand hedge and descend the long field to reach the valley floor. Take the gate in the left-hand corner to enter another field. In the field, keep with the left-hand boundary and head towards a wooden footbridge in the copse ahead. Go through a gate to take the footbridge and through another gate to exit the copse. Enter another field and turn left uphill. Keep to the left-hand hedge of the field and go through a small copse and gate to a lane. Turn left along the lane for about 100 metres. Ignore the green field gate you immediately see off to your right.

C As the lane bends around to the left, take the neighbouring gate immediately ahead. In the field proceed uphill, keep-ing the boundary to your right. Go through two gates to enter and exit a spinney. Stick with the right-hand boundary of the large field as you climb and then contour Priest Barrow on your left. Before reaching crossing electricity lines take a gate in the right-hand hedgerow. In the next field, continue in the same direction, but with the hedgerow now on your left. Follow the path gently uphill along the hedgerow as it curves right and through a gate into another field. Continue uphill with the left-hand boundary and through another gate. You are now skirting the edge of Farmborough Common. In the next field keep with the same boundary and go through a further gate adjacent to a water trough. In the following field keep with the left-hand boundary. Go straight towards a pond in the left-hand corner and follow it round to take a gate ahead into another field. Continue in the same direction towards the left-hand corner of this field, aiming to the left of a house. Exit a gate on to a lane. Turn right on the lane, ignoring the stile in front of you. Proceed downhill for about 200 metres until you reach the valley bottom.

D Here go through a gate off to your left. You now proceed with stream on your left for about 800 metres, passing through three fields and ignoring all bridges off to your left. In the third field the path descends gently downhill to a field gate ahead. Go through this gate, ignoring the bridge off to the left. Continue straight ahead on the fenced track for about 100 metres, with the stream still to your left. In the next field immediately turn left with the track to cross the stream. On the other side, go up the bank and over the waymarked stile in the fence ahead to enter a field. In the field turn right and follow the fence with the stream now on your right. Cross two fields and stiles, with woodland over to the right. In the third field veer away from the stream, climbing diagonally up the hillside and aiming for the top left-hand corner of the field. As you climb, the tower of Priston church gradually comes into view, with impressive views of the valley ahead and down to your right.

E Climb the stile in the corner and proceed along the left-hand hedge of the next field towards a further stile. Over to the right is a stone monument on a knoll, with views back down the valley. Take the stile ahead to pick up a hedged track leading into the village, which soon merges into a lane. Follow the lane past

the church and then straight-ahead towards a T-junction, immediately to the right of the Ring O'Bells. Here turn right on the main village street and go downhill. Keep with the road as it bends round to the left through the village until just before the road curves right and crosses a stream. Here go through a gate to take a path off to the left. Follow the path through an open grassed area towards the entrance of the sewage treatment works. At this point bear left with the path as it proceeds through scrubland past the treatment works. Go ahead through a gate into woodland. Follow the path with the stream to your right; it soon heads uphill and through another gate to exit the woodland.

F Enter a field and continue along the long right-hand boundary, with woodland to your right. Continue with the boundary until a gate appears in the far boundary ahead. Go through the gate to cross a footbridge. Take a further gate to enter another field. Here you bear left uphill. Go through a visible gate up on the far boundary. In the next field continue uphill towards a tree in the middle. Here bear further left and uphill to take a metal kissing-gate in front of farm out-buildings. Proceed along a short fenced path between the buildings to exit by a gate on to a crossing track. Turn left down the hedged track to soon go through a field gate. In the field follow the path downhill immediately to the right of the line of the electricity poles. At the penultimate pole in the field, veer right to take a gate in the hedge. In the next field turn left and within about 50 metres go through a gate.

G Cross a footbridge and go through a further gate to enter a further field. Proceed straight across the field, aiming for a gate immediately in front of Priston Mill, which is clearly visible ahead. Go through the gate and straight ahead on to the gravel driveway. Follow the driveway to pass the mill buildings on your left and to exit on to a lane. Beyond the mill, continue straight along the lane. Ignore a turning off to the left. Proceed gently uphill for about 500 metres until you reach a junction with another lane. Here turn right for about a 100 metres.

H You reach a stone barn on your right. Immediately before the barn take a surfaced track off to the right. Follow the track steeply uphill with the boundary to your left. Enter the next field through a gap. From now on, stay with the right-hand boundary. Keep ahead on the same track as it becomes grassier but continues to climb steeply. Proceed into a third field, in which the gradient lessens. In the fourth field you pass over the brow of the hill. Keep ahead, with the bound-

ary still to your right, and go through a gate on to a road. Cross straight over the road to pick up a narrower continuation of the track, which is more obviously an ancient green lane. Go quite steeply downhill for about 250 metres, passing through a pair of stone pillars. As the track narrows even further, look out for steps up to a gate off to the left.

I Take the steps and go through the gate to follow the path through the copse. Exit via another gate into a field with panoramic views down to Stanton Prior ahead. Descend the hillside diagonally left, keeping alongside the field's boundary with an orchard until reaching the far corner. Just to the left of this corner adjoining the orchard, take a gate to enter the adjacent field. Bear left across the field, to take a gate in a stone wall just to the left of the church. Proceed along a ginnel and through the churchyard. Exit via a gate to access the village street where the walk started. **A**

Tresham, Alderley and Ozleworth

Distance 8.5 miles / 14 kms

Time 4 hours

OS Map Explorer 167

Starting Point Grass verge, centre of the village of Tresham - OS reference 794912

Parking Free parking on grass verge

Reaching the start from Bristol Go east on the M4. Leave by Junction 18 and then go north on the A46. After about seven miles take the left turn to Tresham. In the centre of the village go round a sharp left-hand bend to reach the verge on your left

Refreshments None

THIS WALK is a Cotswolds gem, encompassing woodland, country estates, steep-sided valleys, meandering streams and spectacular views. The terrain is undulating, with a couple of steep climbs. Most of the walk is on tracks and lanes, much of it along the Cotswold Way.

The route starts at the hamlet of Tresham, from where you descend along a stream and valley to pick up the Cotswold Way. You progress up an escarpment with pleasant southerly views to reach the village of Alderley, which includes a number of fine houses built on the legacy of the woollen industry. From Alderley the route descends to cross pasture before a long climb through various woodland, emerging to spectacular panoramic views across the Severn Estuary and towards Wotton-under-Edge. The walk continues along a track to circle the Newark Park estate before soon reaching Ozleworth Park. Ozleworth House is 18th century; the adjacent 12th-century church is reputed to be of pre-Christian origin. From here you descend gently through parkland to Ozleworth Bottom, the site of a long gone woollen mill. From Ozleworth Bottom it is a protracted climb up through woodland and farmland to return to Tresham and the starting point.

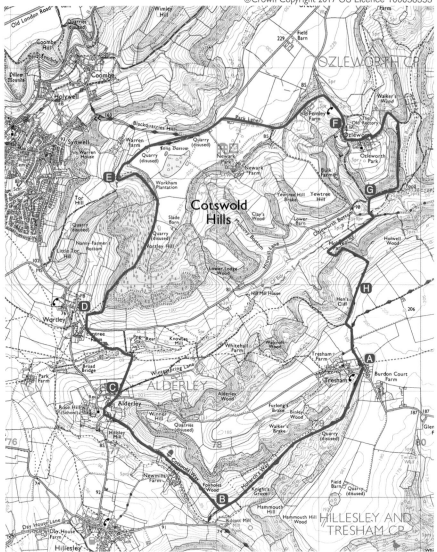

A The walk starts on the green verge in the centre of the village of Tresham. From the green verge take the steps signed down to the Tresham Millenium Garden. Join a grass track, pass the Millennium Garden on your right and head through a field gate. Stick with the grass track as it gradually descends into the valley ahead. After about 300 metres the track bends right. Continue to descend through trees and pass through a gate, as the still-grassy track descends more gradually in an open valley. After a pond on your right, go through another field gate. Continue on the well-defined track, with a stream now on your right.

Go through a further field gate. Beyond this gate, the track is usually muddy. Continue on the now hedged track for about 150 metres.

B Take the right-hand turning through a gate signed for the Cotswold Way. Take the track uphill through trees and through a field gate. Keep with the fenced/hedged track. The terrain levels out and the fenced track emerges via a gate into an open field. Continue alongside the left-hand boundary. Go uphill through successive field gates via an enclosed stretch of track to enter a further field. Carry on along the left-hand edge and, with buildings visible ahead on the horizon, go through successive field gates, 50 metres apart. Continue up the track ahead to pass through a further gate. Within about a 100 metres, the track becomes a driveway serving several houses. Continue on the driveway until you reach a road junction, with Alderley church ahead of you. At the junction, turn right and then immediately take the lane off to the right, following the clear Cotswold Way waymarks through the village. Proceed downhill on the lane to reach the crossroads. Go straight ahead on the lane for about another 50 metres.

C Take the left-hand fork. Head down the sunken track with trees on either side. At the bottom, as another footpath joins from the right, bear left with the track. Cross the stream over a stone bridge, go through a field gate and then cross a narrow field to go through another gate. After briefly keeping to the left-hand boundary, follow the waymarks to cross diagonally to the right-hand corner of the long field, passing beneath

power lines to exit via a gate on to a lane. Cross the lane and go through another gate to pick up the track opposite. Follow this for 100 metres.

D Take a gate on your right to enter woodland. Proceed up the banked path. Keep climbing on this steep stony path. The gradient gradually becomes gentler and you reach a clearing where other tracks join. Continue with the way-marked track straight uphill, remaining in the woodland and ignoring the turns off to the left and right. After about a further 100 metres take the left-hand fork. Carry on uphill on the track for about a further 500 metres until the gradient begins to level out. Ignore an unmarked track off to the left and continue until you reach a clearly marked path off to the left. Go down the stepped path to a gate. Take this to emerge from the woodland. Initially

follow the contours and the left-hand boundary of the field for about 200 metres before heading uphill towards a seat in the top corner, with panoramic views.

E At the field corner turn right and follow the right hand wall to a field gate. Pass through the gate and on to a much more defined track. Follow this walled/ tree-lined track for about 300 metres all the way to the road, including a final short section in parallel with the road. Upon reaching the road turn right. You shortly pass a cottage, which is part of the Newark Park estate. Continue on the road in the same direction for about a further 150 metres, with the Newark Park estate boundary on your right. Take the first lane off to the right, continuing with the estate boundary on your right. Upon reaching the entrance of Newark

Park, continue ahead downhill on the same lane through trees. You descend to pass Fernley Farm and its main driveway before going ahead to reach a T-junction. Turn right and follow the lane past the pillar-box and telephone-box for about 150 metres until you reach two houses ahead, on the edge of the Ozleworth Park estate.

F Take the footpath between the houses and enter Ozleworth Park. Follow the path as it joins the drive and then swings round to the left, eventually passing Ozleworth Church (which you can take a short diversion to visit off to the right), to reach a pond on the left. After the pond the path curves right to link up with the driveway to Ozleworth Park Farm. Here turn left and follow the metalled driveway for about 200 metres before taking the right-hand fork. Follow this track downhill to cross a cattle-grid. Continue to follow the track for about a further 100 metres as it curves right and downhill until you reach a right-hand fork leading gently back uphill. Take this undulating track, which soon picks up the right-hand edge of woodland ahead. Descend gently to go through a field gate and enter the woodland. Continue uphill and then briefly downhill as the track curves around to the right before joining a crossing track. Here turn right and continue gently uphill within the woodland for about 100 metres until just past a seat, the track emerges into the open, with a sloping field appearing down on the left. Keep with the track as it carries on alongside the field.

G Go through a small gate in the black railings at the end of the field on the left. Head down the field steeply towards the bottom right hand corner, where you cross a stile on to the road to reach Ozleworth Bottom. Go straight ahead on the road, passing the cottages on the left and crossing the stream. Keep with the road as it bends right and uphill. Continue climbing until you take a farm gate. Proceed ahead in front of Holwell Farm and pass through another similar gate. Carry on ahead on the tree-lined footpath in the same direction for about 150 metres before bending sharp left with the far boundary to reach a metal field gate after about a further 50 metres. Enter woodland and climb steadily upwards on a track between banks to go through a further field gate. Exit the woodland into a field and continue with the woodland now on your left. Stick with the left-hand boundary as the terrain opens up and as the track contin-

ues to climb. The track bends round to the right with the boundary, and proceeds towards and through a red painted field gate.

H You now join a fenced track. Continue ahead on this, still climbing, albeit much more gently, until you go through a further red painted gate. Turn left and continue on the fenced track for about 200 metres. Ignore all turns off to the left and right until, as the village of Tresham comes into view, the track curves sharply to the right. You soon reach a farm gate on the left, which you take to enter a field. Follow the footpath across the field, heading for a stone stile just to the right of the buildings immediately ahead of you. Take the stile and follow the footpath round to the left through the private gardens. Turn right on to the driveway, which leads out on to the road. At the road turn right and you are back to the grass verge where you started the walk. **A**

Charterhouse and Compton Martin

Distance 8 miles / 13 kms

Time 4 to 4.5 hours

OS Map Explorer 141

Starting Point Blackmoor Nature Reserve, Charterhouse - OS reference 505557

Parking Free at Blackmoor Nature Reserve car park - other options nearby

Reaching the start from Bristol Take the A38 south from Bristol and past the airport to Churchill. At Churchill turn left on A368 to Bath. After about two miles take the right-hand turn on the B3134 through Burrington Combe. After about three miles turn right to Charterhouse. At Charterhouse turn left at the crossroads in front of the AONB Centre. Go down the lane to the car park

Refreshments Ring O'Bells, Compton Martin

THIS WALK provides spectacular views of Blagdon Lake and Chew Valley Lake; fascinating industrial archaeology; the Blackmoor Nature Reserve; the village of Compton Martin and diverse woodland. Much of the terrain is undemanding but there is one steep descent and a similar climb. The walk is mainly on tracks and well-defined footpaths.

The walk starts at Charterhouse in the heart of the Mendip Hills. The relics of the lead mining industry, of pre-Roman origin, are apparent in the ponds and spoil heaps you soon traverse. This area is within the wider Blackmoor Nature Reserve – supporting a diversity of plants, fauna and birds. You progress up Rains Batch heading over fields in the broad direction of Blagdon. Spectacular views soon open up ahead. The route then takes the ancient track of Leaze Lane along the escarpment, with further continuous views. From here you pass through the recently planted Hazel Manor Woods. The route descends through the more mature Compton Wood to reach Compton Martin, which has a pretty pond and a fine church. You climb back through Compton Wood and Hazel Manor Woods. From here the route eventually reaches Nether Wood, an important part of the Blackmoor Nature Reserve. Through and beyond you pass other signs of the area's industrial past, including derelict flues, before returning to the start.

A From the parking area, take the main track northwards, away from the entrance. Soon bear left between two metal posts. In about a further 150 metres take a clear path off to the left down steps. Follow the path down to a pond. Keep to the left of the pond and take a stile in the fence ahead of you. Enter a field and proceed with the wall on your left until you cross a stile on to the road. At the road turn right. Proceed for about 150 metres until taking a lane off to the left. Proceed uphill for about 200 metres, passing a bungalow on your left and through two metal posts on either side of the road.

B Immediately after the metal posts, take a stile on the right to enter an open field. In the field bear diagonally left and uphill towards the right-hand edge of some obvious earthworks. Upon reaching the earthworks, follow along their outer edge in a similar direction. Before reaching the end of the field strike out downhill to take a stile in the far right-hand corner of the field. In the next field continue downhill. Keep to the left-hand hedge to enter a further field via a gateway in the corner. From here proceed in the direction of the farm-house ahead, keeping within range of the left-hand edge of the field and aiming for the left-hand corner. Go through the gate. Climb up the field on what is now a clear track, with the farm-house on your left. Go through a field gate to reach the main road. Cross the main road to take the Blagdon Road just ahead of you. Proceed initially uphill on the road but then descend for about 350 metres, as views of Blagdon Lake and Chew Valley Lake open out ahead.

C Take Leaze Lane, the first right-hand turning. Continue ahead on Leaze Lane

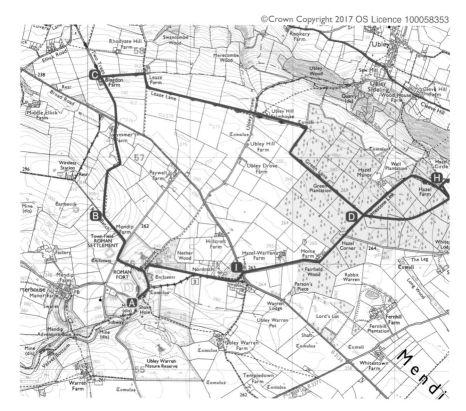

until you reach a crossing track, just before the farm ahead on your left. Turn right up the hedged track. Keep uphill for about 100 metres until you reach the corner. Here follow the track as it curves round to the left and begins to rise much less steeply. Keep with the hedged track as it gradually climbs the hillside, with panoramic views off to the left. Stay with the track for at least 800 metres until you reach a gate. Take the gate into a field, where you keep with the left-hand hedge until reaching a gate leading out on to a lane. Cross the lane and continue ahead in the same direction, now on a hedged stony track. Pass Ubley Hill Farmhouse on your left to go through a gate. After this the track becomes grassier. Continue gently uphill with the walled track as it

goes round a right-hand bend, passing a fine line of beeches. Continue over a stile by a gate and stick with the track as it bends around to the left. With Hazel Manor Woods now on your left, continue straight ahead for 800 metres or so on the hedged track towards a junction of tracks.

D Take a stile at the junction. Immediately turn left and go through a hunting gate on to a drive with an avenue of beech trees. Almost immediately take a stile by the fourth tree on the right. Follow the well-defined path for about 800 metres as it wends its way through the planted woodland. Continue ahead, avoiding all crossing paths. Eventually a further panoramic view of Chew Valley

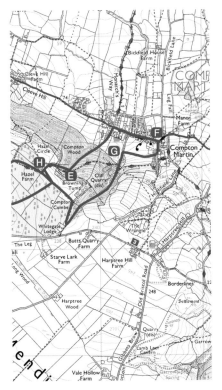

in the right-hand corner. Continue through a gate to emerge on a driveway, which after about 100 metres reaches a junction with the main road, The Street. Turn right along The Street to pass the Ring O'Bells pub. Continue along The Street, past a junction on the right and within about 100 metres climb a road straight up ahead to reach the Church of St Michael the Archangel. The church has views to the village pond opposite.

F From the church, head back down to the Street and cross the road by the pond. Continue along The Street for a further 100 metres in the same direction as before. Then cross back again to take Rectory Lane. Go up Rectory Lane for about 100 metres before taking a gate off to the right, opposite to The Gables. Enter the field and follow the right-hand boundary of the churchyard. Then keep straight ahead in the same direction across the field towards the house furthest to the right. You eventually go through a gate just to the left of this house.

G Turn left up the metalled lane to pass several houses. After passing Hazelwood Cottage, the last house on the left, ignore the crossing path. Keep on straight-ahead as the lane becomes a track and then a path. Keep with the path as it meanders and climbs, sometimes steeply, passing through a disused quarry. After crossing a stile keep uphill with the path. After about a further 200 metres climbing through mossy boulders, the path begins to follow a fence on its left-hand edge. As you continue uphill within the woodland ignore a gate off to the left. Beyond here a field becomes visible over to your left. Keep

Lake opens up ahead and you reach a stile by a gate. Cross the stile and turn left. Bear left towards the metal field gate, just to the right of Hazel Farm. Do not go through the gate, instead turn right alongside the wall. At the end of the wall, bear sharply right to go steeply downhill towards a hunting gate into woodland. Once in the woodland continue for about 100 metres until you see a waymark post off to the right.

E Take the waymarked path going down to the left. Proceed on a steep and prolonged descent. Be careful as it can be slippery. Continue until you eventually exit the woodland into a field via a gate, with Compton Martin visible ahead. Bear right down the field to take a stile

uphill with the path until reaching a T-junction of paths. A house is up to the left but you turn right. Follow a level path between the fenced boundary of the planted woodland, Hazel Manor Woods, which you traversed earlier in the walk, and the more established woodland that you have just been in. Keep along the path and after about 250 metres, take a hunting gate off to the left to enter a field. Proceed uphill in the field along the right-hand boundary wall for about 100 metres before passing through a gap into another field. Now keep to the left-hand side of the same boundary. Continue uphill until the familiar sight of Hazel Farm appears ahead. Continue with the hedge immediately to your left to pass the stile you took in exiting the woods earlier in the walk. Do not retrace your footsteps to Hazel Farm exactly. This time keep with the left-hand hedge towards the left-hand-corner of the field, to the left of the farm.

H Take the stile and go diagonally left across the grass verge adjacent the farm to pick up the metalled driveway. Proceed gently uphill on the fenced driveway, with woodland on each side, for about 200 metres until reaching a T-junction of tracks. Turn left and continue ahead on the surfaced track. Go through a gateway and then through the avenue of beech trees to reach the gateway and junction of tracks at the main entrance into Hazel Manor Woods that you encountered previously. This time you continue straight ahead along the driveway until passing through successive gates at Hazel Lodge to exit on to a minor road. Here turn right to continue in the same direction. Continue ahead along the

road for a further 1000 metres or so until you reach the B3134.

I Cross the road and take the surfaced track immediately opposite, to the right of Nordrach Lodge and a pillar box. Stick with the surfaced track as it bends round to the right into woodland, now in parallel with another track, which is also a right of way. Continue straight ahead on the surfaced track, passing by various buildings on the right. When the track divides go ahead on the grassy track, soon taking a field gate. Still within woodland, continue on a fenced path before going through a further gate to enter Nether Wood. Continue ahead on the main path through Nether Wood keeping to the left-hand boundary wall, and passing various remains of flues and buildings on route. Upon exiting the wood, just beyond a seat, you reach a crossing path. Turn left and proceed on this path, with the ponds you traversed at the beginning of the walk now down to your right. Keep ahead until finally reaching the car park. **A**

East Harptree, Hinton Blewett and Coley

Distance 9 miles / 14.5 kms

Time 5 to 5.5 hours

OS Map Explorer 141

Starting Point East Harptree Woods car park - OS reference 557542

Parking Free parking in East Harptree Woods car park

Reaching the start from Bristol Take the A37 out of Bristol through Pensford and turn right on the A368 through Bishop Sutton to reach West Harptree. Here turn left towards East Harptree and then take the right-hand turn to and through the village. Continue towards the top of the hill out of East Harptree for about a mile and the car park is on the right

Refreshments Ring O'Bells, Hinton Blewett and just before Hinton Blewett, a picnic seat with panoramic views

---

THIS MENDIP WALK blends panoramic views, rolling countryside, industrial archaeology, a secluded combe of natural interest and a historic village. Although some of the terrain is flat, this is a demanding walk, including a prolonged climb at the end; also Harptree Combe can be tricky to traverse in the winter.

The walk starts in the mainly coniferous woodland of East Harptree Woods. Your first destination is Smitham Chimney, a 19th-century relic of thousands of years of lead-mining on Mendip. Exiting the woodland and with panoramic views soon opening up, the route continues down towards and through Harptree Combe; which is full of interesting flowers and trees and especially attractive in the spring. You pass by the derelict Richmont Castle and a water aqueduct. The route then goes across the Chew Valley, crossing the river at Shrowl Bridge. There follows a steep climb to Prospect Stile with its extensive views across Mendip and beyond. The circle then bears towards Hinton Blewett, which has an interesting church and village green. From here you descend Coley Hill, past the reservoir. From Coley there follows a prolonged climb through attractive fields and woodland. There are further panoramic views as the route circles back to its start.

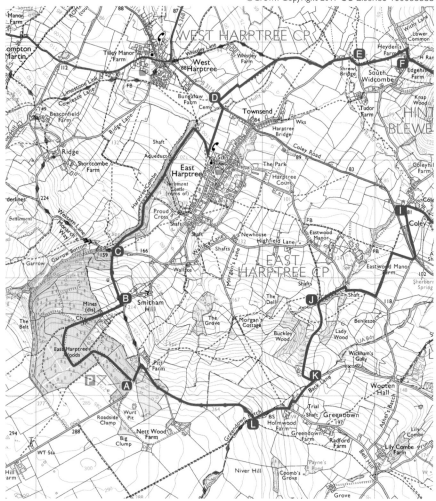

A From the entrance of the car park turn left along the forest track and through the green barrier. When you reach a seat on your right, ignore a crossing path and continue with the track as it curves around to the left for about a further 150 metres until you reach a clearly signed path off to the right. Take this surfaced path and descend gently through woodland until you reach Smitham Pond, with Smitham Chimney beyond. Follow the path ahead around the pond to reach a junction of paths by the chimney. Turn right to pass the chimney on your right. Follow the track gently downhill through further woodland to go through a gate. Pick up the fenced track straight ahead and go down it for about 150 metres. Immediately after going through a gate turn left to take the fenced track off to the left.

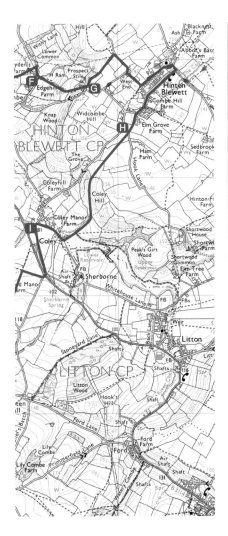

a lane at the bottom. Turn left along the lane for about 100 metres. Just before reaching a farm on your left, take the gate off to your right. Bear right and keep level (not straight and uphill) across the field towards the woodland.

C Go through a gate to enter Harptree Combe. Follow the path and the stream down the combe. Carry on down the combe, which can be very muddy. You will need to criss-cross the stream to avoid getting stuck in the mud. When in doubt, aim to keep on the left-hand side of the stream. Follow waymarks down the combe and pass the ruins of Richmont Castle on your right. When a water culvert appears on your right, follow the line of this. Beyond here continue on the path until you reach steps leading down to a crossing track. At this junction turn left and continue further down the combe, with the stream now on your left. There are high stone walls on the right supporting the water pipeline. Eventually the path curves with the stream away to the right, passing beneath the pipeline. From here continue with the path alongside the stream for a further 250 metres or so until exiting via a stile at the end of the combe. In the field turn right and proceed uphill between hedges to cross a further stile. In the next field keep with hedge on your left, in the direction of East Harptree church tower. Look out for a metal field gate on your left. Turn sharp left through the field gate and proceed downhill, away from East Harptree, keeping to the left-hand fence. Go through the field gate at the bottom to enter the next field, where you head downhill to a gate in the left-hand

B After about 50 metres, go straight through a gate ahead to enter a field. Proceed down the centre of the field and through a gate in the far hedge. In the next field skirt a big hollow off to the right and aim for the far right corner. Cross two successive gates through the corner of woodland and into a further field. In the field, follow the left-hand boundary downhill, walking adjacent to the woodland to go through a gate on to

corner adjacent to a cemetery. Go over the stile on the gate to reach a road. Here turn left and proceed for about 50 metres.

D Take a turn off to the right through a gate. In the field keep towards the left–hand hedge to cross a stile, about 50 metres to the right of the corner. The next field is long. Continue in the same direction, still along the left edge, to pick up a stile at the bottom of the field as it narrows. Take the stile to reach a cross-ing track. Go ahead and bear right to cross a stone bridge and another stile. In the next field follow the left-hand boundary and keep with it, ignoring a turn off to the left via a gate. Eventually you reach a gate in the far corner by an oak tree. Go through this gate and turn left along the lane. You soon reach the hamlet of Shrowl Bridge. Continue along the lane. After passing cottages, cross two bridges over the river. Just after the second of these, a stone bridge, look out for a stile on your left.

E Take the stile and then immediately to your left cross a plank bridge into a field. Follow the edge of the stream to the right-hand corner. Go through two successive gates to reach another field, in which you head for the far left corner. Go through the gate, over a plank bridge and turn right, aiming for a gate between a pylon and a stone barn. Go through this and bear right across the next field towards a gate. Go through the gate, down the steps and cross the verge on to a lane. Turn right and proceed for about 100 metres.

F Look out for a waymark off to the left. Go through the gate and proceed uphill

towards the incomplete hedgerow rolling down the hillside ahead of you. Once you reach the hedgerow, keep to the right of it and climb steeply to go through a gate. In the next field continue to climb in the same direction. Go through another gate to join a path coming in from the right. Continue straight ahead steeply uphill through scrubland as the path curves up into a field. Once in the field bear left sharply. Head up towards and through a gate in the top corner of the field to reach a well-known view-point, Prospect Stile.

G There is a seat from which to enjoy the views, with a photographic montage to explain them. From Prospect Stile turn left down the wooded track. After emerg-ing into the open, proceed for about a further 50 metres towards a crossing track. Immediately before reaching the track turn right through a gate (easily

missed) into a paddock area. Follow a path alongside the left-hand hedge. Cross a stile and bear slightly right to cross a further stile into a stable yard. Cross the yard to take a further stile into a lane. Go straight ahead on the lane and continue with it as it bends left past houses to reach Hinton Blewett church, and beyond this to the village green, where the Ring O'Bells is situated. From the pub cross the green, bearing right towards the telephone box, and then turn right to follow the Lower Road. Continue down this road through the village to its furthest edge, where you turn left into Hook Lane. Proceed for about 200 metres, passing a playground, before looking out on the right for a stile by a gate.

H Take the stile to enter a field. Bear left across the field to take a stile in the boundary ahead. In the next field keep ahead in a similar direction, but veering slightly to the right to cross a further stile in the boundary. In the field beyond start to descend Coley Hill, curving diagonally left and keeping the telegraph poles to your right. Go through a gate to enter a large field. Initially head on down in the same direction towards a large oak tree, with Coley Lower Reservoir becoming visible in the distance. Proceed on the indistinct path just past this oak and then keep to the left of another oak. From here continue diagonally down the field towards a further oak in the far right-hand corner. Beyond the oak go through a metal gate. Turn immediately sharp right down the next field keeping to the hedgerow. Head for a gate at the bottom, visible in front of the reservoir. Go through the gate and down the steps to reach Coley Lower Reservoir. Go straight ahead to cross the dam and an iron-railed bridge. Go over a cattle grid and through a gate. Bear right along the track, continuing past a farm to reach a lane in the village of Coley.

I Turn left up the lane, signed to Litton, following it uphill between high-sided banks all the way up to the main road. At the main road turn right for about 100 metres before taking the first lane off to the left. Immediately up to the right at this junction are steps to a marked footpath. Go up to the steps to take a gate into a field. Follow the left-hand hedge and go through a gate to enter another field. Here turn sharp left and continue to follow the left-hand boundary. Go through a gate. In the next field continue in the same direction through a further gate in the left-hand corner on to a lane. Turn right along the lane for about 350 metres, passing a footpath off to the left before reaching a pair of cottages down to the right.

J Go through a metal gate opposite the cottages to take the footpath off to the left into a field. Follow it as it curves steeply and rightwards up the field. Go through another metal gate in the hedgerow. In the next field turn left with the left-hand boundary. At the field corner turn right with the boundary. Head uphill, keeping adjacent with woodland. In the far left-hand corner you reach a T-junction with a wooded track in the corner of the woodland. Proceed left, immediately exiting the woodland via a gate into an open field. In the field a house is visible immediately ahead. Initially bear slightly left up the field towards further woodland but eventually curve back to the right to enter a copse at the top of the field, with the house now over to your right. In the copse follow the stream on your left and cross it to enter another field. Head up the right-hand side of the field with woodland to your right. In the top right corner go through a gap into another field and up the fence line. In the corner, with a house over on the right, turn left. Still in the field, carry on along the fence line to reach the next corner. Go out through the field gate and down to a lane.

K Turn right on the lane and keep uphill with it as it curves left and right for about 300 metres. You pass a large house and follow its wall on the left before reaching a T-junction, with Holmwood Farm immediately ahead. Here turn right, and then take the track ahead, leading uphill into woodland. The stony track soon curves away to the left. Keep with the wooded track for about 250 metres as it continues uphill until you reach a very clearly waymarked metal gate on your right. Exit the woodland through the gate and into a field.

L Proceed up the field along the right-hand edge, in the direction of a gap in the hedge in the corner. Go through into the next field and here curve leftwards along the hillside, as panoramic views of Chew Valley Lake open up over to your right and with an impressive line of beech trees along the left-hand field boundary. Take a stile about 50 metres down from the left-hand corner of the field. Continue along the next field, closing in gradually towards the left-hand boundary and through a field gate in the top left-hand corner. Continue along the

fenced track and through a further gate. Here the track joins the main driveway for Nettwood Farm. Keep with the surfaced driveway for about 250 metres, initially through woodland and then with further open views across the Chew Valley, all the way down to the road. At the road, turn left uphill for about 100 metres until you reach a right-hand junction into the car park where you started. **A**

Oakhill and Maesbury Castle

Distance 7.5 miles / 12 kms

Time 3.5 hours

OS Map Explorer 142

Starting Point Oakhill Inn, Oakhill - OS reference 635473

Parking Free on-street parking at the eastern end of the High Street near to the Oakhill Inn

Reaching the start from Bristol Take the A37 out of Bristol and continue through Pensford, Farrington Gurney, Ston Easton and Gurney Slade. About a mile beyond Gurney Slade take the sharp left-hand turn on to the A367. Proceed for about a mile to reach the centre of Oakhill

Refreshments Oakhill Inn, Oakhill

THIS WALK explores the open Mendip countryside to the north of Shepton Mallet, taking in the pleasant village of Oakhill, high quality woodland, Roman roads, Iron-Age and Roman fortifications – including the spectacular earthworks of Maesbury Castle – and panoramic views. The terrain is undulating, with a couple of short but sharp climbs. The route mainly follows tracks and quiet country lanes. There is one potentially muddy stretch.

From Oakhill the route soon picks up the alignment of the old Fosse Way. You follow this through Beacon Hill Wood comprising mixed woodland, now managed by the Woodland Trust, and former quarries with nearby evidence of both Iron-Age and Roman occupation. The walk goes on to traverse stone stiles across pleasant farmland with views across to Glastonbury Tor. You continue along a quiet country lane passing a historic mill complex before picking up the ancient track of Burnthouse Lane. You bear in the direction of the Iron-Age Maesbury Castle, which you steeply climb. You should be rewarded by spectacular panoramic views. The scenic descent eventually leads you to link up with the ancient track of Limehouse Lane. The walk now heads back towards Oakhill, concluding via an interesting detour arounds its northern edge, and then back to the centre and the start.

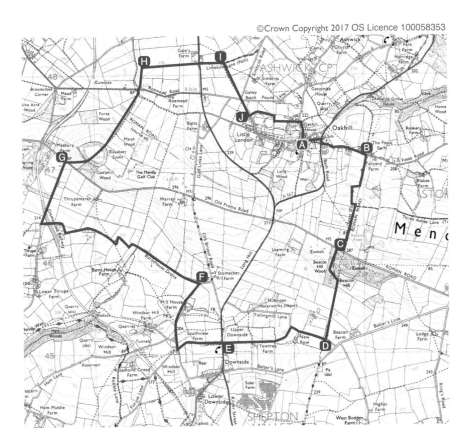

A From the High Street, head towards the Oakhill Inn and cross the A367. Immediately take the road opposite, Fosse Road, passing the inn on your left. Proceed with care along this road for about 400 metres until you reach Park Farm on your left. Just past Park Farm and opposite to Fosse Toll Cottage, is a track off to the right.

B Take this wooded track and proceed straight ahead. You are now on part of the Fosse Way, the old Roman road. Follow the track uphill, initially in the expected straight-line. As the track becomes more wooded and sunken follow it around to the right and then left around what was probably a fort.

After passing the fort you revert to the earlier alignment, avoiding paths off to the left and right. Continue in a straight-line uphill along the wooded track until you reach the road.

C Cross the road and immediately enter Beacon Hill Wood via a gap in the fence. Note that the woodland, which is managed by the Woodland Trust, is open access, so you need not rely on defined paths. Immediately turn right and follow the perimeter adjacent to the road for about 100 metres to pick up the main track entrance to the woods from the road. The main track (which you will pick up again shortly) goes straight-ahead deep into the woodland. However, you should take the right-hand fork which leads in about a further 100 metres to a seat and viewing point. At this point bear left away from the road but as you proceed downhill keep within about 50 metres of the perimeter of the woodland. Within about 200 metres the main track (see above) will appear on your left. Link up with this. Proceed gradually downhill until you reach the boundary fence ahead. Here curve right with track and reconnect with the alignment of the old Fosse Way. Continue ahead out of the woodland and along the wooded track for about 600 metres until you reach a metal barrier and road.

D Turn right and continue along the undulating road, passing a pillar box on your right. Past New Row Farm on your left continue uphill for about a further 100 metres. Look out for a gate and stile to your left. As you climb the stile, on a clear day, you can see Glastonbury Tor ahead in the distance. Bear right towards the corner of the field, keeping to the right of a line of telegraph poles until you reach the last one. The stone stile you are looking out for is 20 metres to the left of this telegraph pole. Take the stile and proceed with the boundary to your left through two fields, crossing a further stone stile (with additional wooden stiles on each side). When you reach farm buildings on your left cross the stile and then turn left through a gate and turn right, now to follow the right-hand boundary. Cross a wooden stepped stile and continue ahead in the same direction to reach and cross a stile at the edge of the A37.

E Cross the A37 with care and pick up the track almost immediately opposite. Go over a stile and, keeping to the right-hand boundary, head towards disused farm buildings. Glastonbury Tor is usually visible again to your left. Carry on through the farmyard. In the field beyond, keep to the left-hand boundary to pick up a stile in the left-hand corner, which only becomes visible upon immediate approach. In the next field, again keep to the left-hand boundary until you reach and cross a stone stile out on to a lane. Turn right and continue on the lane for about 800 metres as it undulates up and down; climbing to Quarry House on the left, descending to Mill House Farm and various other buildings on the right and then climbing back uphill towards Fern Cottage, which becomes directly visible ahead.

F At the cottage turn left along the hedged no-through road. Proceed all the way until reaching a field gate immediately ahead, where the drive to Burnt House Farm leads off to the left. Go ahead through the gate and follow the enclosed track as it weaves left and right until you reach a field gate across it. Go through the gate and follow the path through the next two fields. Keep to the left-hand boundary in the first field. Go through a gate and then head for the right-hand edge of the woodland straight ahead in the second. At the end of the second field you reach a further field gate in the left-hand corner. Go through this on to a wooded/ hedged track and after about 150 metres you reach a lane. Turn right and proceed straight up the lane for about 600 metres. The hillside of Maesbury Castle becomes increasingly evident ahead. Eventually you reach a T-junction. Here turn right and after about 50 metres cross the road to a stile on the opposite side of the road.

G Go over the stile and bear right to climb steeply up the field in the direction of a field gate in top right-hand corner. Here climb the stile to enter the curtilage of Maesbury Castle. Immediately after the stile, turn sharply left to take a path leading up to the top of the earthworks. Turn right and do an almost exact half-circuit of the earthworks. Look out for a clear path leading down to a group of trees and a gate. Go through this gate and shortly another one before emerging into a field to immediately pass an impressive line of beech trees. Descend through the next two fields, via another gate, keeping to the left-hand boundary. After entering the next field through a further gate, keep to the right-hand hedge as far it runs, then continue ahead in the same direction, now following a stream on your right, towards the far boundary. You turn right at this boundary and keep it to your left to cross the stream and reach a stile in the far left-hand corner. Take this stone stile and continue boundary right to reach the road via another stone stile.

H Cross the road directly to Roemead Lane. Go along Roemead Lane for about 200 metres until, as it begins to curve left, an easily missed stile appears in the hedgerow. Take this stile and proceed uphill to another stile ahead. Cross this into Limekiln Lane, a broad hedged/wooded track. Follow this track for about 500 metres until you reach the A37. Cross the A37 and proceed along

Limekiln Lane for about a further 200 metres in a straight line. Just as the track begins to deviate to the left and immediately in front of a small copse, look out for an easily missed stone stile in the right-hand boundary.

I Take the stile and proceed through the next field with the boundary to your left to cross another stone stile. In the next field continue with the boundary to your left until you reach a field gate. Exit the field gate to reach a crossroads. At the crossroads take Galley Batch Lane, signed to Oakhill. Proceed for about 100 metres until on the left and opposite the first properties you reach a signed footpath.

J Go over the stone stile. Keep with the right-hand boundary through the first field to pass through a gap into a further field. Stay with the right-hand boundary in the second field until you reach an

unusual concrete stile. Go through the immediately adjacent gap to take a track which immediately curves sharply to the right through a copse. Proceed for about 100 metres and then go through a gate to bend sharp left. Continue straight ahead on what is now a narrow fenced footpath, edged by a tall coniferous hedge, to reach the built-up area of Oakhill. Keep with the footpath as it emerges on to a driveway with properties on either side. Continue in the same direction to eventually reach a road. Turn right and proceed for about 100 metres until you reach Dean Lane, which forks left downhill. At the bottom of Dean Lane, you bear left down Zion Hill to emerge into the High Street, near to where you started. **A**

Christon and Bleadon

Distance 7.5 miles / 12 kms

Time 3.5 to 4 hours

OS Map Explorer 153

Starting Point Church of St Mary, Banwell Road, Christon - OS reference 379573

Parking Free on-street parking near the church – be careful to park responsibly

Reaching the start from Bristol Follow the A38 south out of Bristol and beyond the Airport, Churchill and Sidcot. Half a mile beyond the A371 junction off to the left, take the right-hand turn to Cross. Continue through Cross and Webbington and over the M5 to reach Loxton. At Loxton keep with the road as it curves to the right, ignoring the road straight-ahead to Weston, to eventually reach Christon

Refreshments Queens Arms, Bleadon

THIS WALK explores the western edge of the Mendip Hills, to the west of the M5, which has a distinct character. At various points the walk encompasses memorable views towards Crook Peak, Brent Knoll, the Somerset Levels, Brean Down, Weston-super-Mare and across the Severn Estuary. The hamlet of Christon and village of Bleadon are each of historic interest. The walk is undulating; and there are a few prolonged climbs. Walking is on tracks and footpaths; one section can be muddy.

From the church at Christon the route climbs up Flagstaff Hill, where spectacular views appear in all directions. Over the hill you soon pick up an ancient crossing track, passing through Christon Plantation before diverting up Shiplate Slait. There are continuous views of Brent Knoll and the Somerset Levels as you descend to reach the hamlet of Shiplate and the River Axe. There follows a walk along the valley and a short climb up to the village of Bleadon, which has origins dating back to the Iron Age and in mediaeval times was a port. From Bleadon the walk climbs Bleadon Hill gradually through scrubland; and then across a golf course towards Hutton Hill, with further panoramic views. There follows a woodland section through to the hamlet of Upper Canada, from which the route climbs back up to Christon Plantation, which you traversed earlier. From here, there is a short descent on a wooded lane taking you back to Christon and the start.

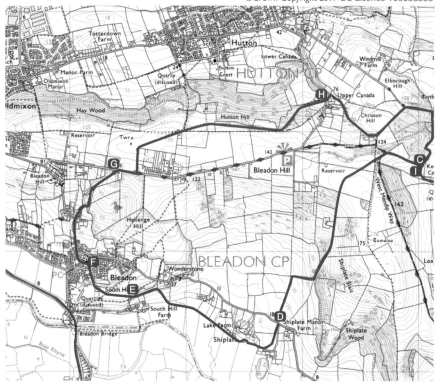

A Before you start, St Mary's church, which is of Norman origin, is worth a visit. From the church take Flagstaff Road, a no-through road immediately at its side. Proceed gently uphill as the road soon becomes a surfaced track. Go straight ahead through a field gate with a house on the right. Continue past the house to cross a stile. From here the track becomes sunken and grassy. Continue uphill and through a gate into an open field. In the field follow the track as it winds gently uphill, initially keeping close to the copse/hedge on your left. As the track becomes more distinct, follow it away from the boundary and more steeply uphill. Eventually you cross a stile next to a field gate at the top of the field.

B Enter the next field and continue on the same track, keeping to the right-hand boundary. You pass over the brow of the hill and views of Weston-super-Mare and beyond appear ahead. Continue downhill to take a stile and join a wooded crossing track. Turn left along this well-defined and ancient track. This can in places be extremely muddy – but fortunately there are less muddy options through the adjoining scrub. Ahead of a junction of tracks is Christon Plantation. Turn left at the junction and continue gradually uphill (with a possible further detour into the woodland to avoid the mud) until you reach cottages on the left, looking out for the third of these, Keepers Cottage.

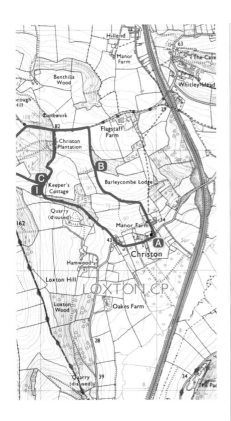

right. Go through another gate, where it becomes enclosed. Continue downhill and through a further gate to join a metalled lane past Hillfield Farm off to the right. Follow the lane downhill. Continue round a sharp left-hand bend, and keep ahead all the way down the hill to the junction with the Loxton-Bleadon road, with Brent Knoll ahead of you on the horizon. Go straight across the road to the Shiplate Fishery. Head into the main entrance for about five metres and immediately look for the gate off to the right.

D Go through the gate into a field. Proceed along the left-hand fence. At the end of the field curve right with the boundary towards a gate in the corner, to the right of a group of cottages. Go through the gate and keep with the left-hand hedge through rough vegetation to reach a footbridge. Cross the footbridge over a stream, and go through a gate to enter a large field. Turn right to follow the stream and the right-hand hedge. Keep with the right-hand hedge to go through a gap and over a rhyne into a further field. Stay with the right-hand hedge and go through a metal gate in the corner of the following field. Go over another bridge to cross another rhyne.

C Do not continue ahead. Instead turn right up another track. Proceed uphill, with Christon Plantation and then a field on your right until you reach a junction off to the left. Take the track up to the left marked the West Mendip Way. After about 100 metres the tracks divide again. Here take the right fork to continue uphill. Carry on up the hedged track until you reach a gate at the end. Go through the gate into the field. Bear right across the field taking the well-defined path towards a gate adjacent to woodland. You are at the top of Shiplate Shait. Here there are panoramic views towards Brent Knoll and the Somerset Levels. Go through the gate. Follow the path as it descends with the fence on your

Head across the next field and through a further gate to cross yet another rhyne. Continue in the same direction through the next three fields. Keep following the right-hand boundary and go ahead through metal gates. Upon leaving the third field, you can see South Hill Farm about 200 metres directly ahead, with a gate immediately in front of you. Do not take this; instead take the gate off to your right into a field. Bear left up the field through a gate in the top boundary to enter a copse. Turn left in the copse. Proceed with the field boundary now on your left. At the end of the copse South Hill Farm is immediately below on your left. You need to take the gate off to the right to enter a further field.

E In the next field, follow the path steeply up the left-hand fenced boundary. Once in the open bear left uphill to join another path and through a gate into a larger open area. Go straight ahead along the hillside until you reach a crossroads of tracks. Here turn right and head uphill. As you climb, Bleadon church appears on the horizon – this is your next destination. Follow the track towards the left-hand corner of the field. Go through successive gates to exit. Then continue on path down steps and through a copse to reach the edge of Bleadon. Go through an iron gate and continue along the now tightly enclosed path until you reach the churchyard.

F Bear left across the front of the church. Exit the churchyard by the main entrance. Pass the old stone village cross to reach Coronation Road. Turn right up the road and then bear left up Celtic Way to pass the Queens Arms on your left. Continue uphill all the way until the road curves around to the left. Turn right immediately after Clovercot. Then

immediately take the marked footpath up the drive off to the left. Proceed past Hellenge House and Dring House over to the right. Here look out for a highly misleading footpath sign (signposted to Combe Martin, Ilfracombe and Barnstaple when I last passed!). Go through the gate ahead to enter a copse. Proceed uphill through the copse with the boundary on your left. Go through a gate at the top and turn left into an open area. Now keep straight ahead in the direction of scrubland, staying within about 50 metres of, and parallel to, the right-hand fence. Follow the prominent waymark into the scrubland. Keep with the path as it winds along, up stone steps and through a further gate off to the left. You soon exit the scrubland into a large field. Climb diagonally up the large field, which is interspersed with further pockets of scrub. Eventually you take a gate in the

top corner leading out on to what is known locally as the Roman Road.

G Turn right up the road until you reach Bleadon Hill Golf Club on your left. Proceed on the road past the hedged enclosure on the left with a seat to reach the furthest extent of the golf course. Here, take the track leading off to the left. Keep with the track, passing the golf club reception on your left. You pass through a gate to reach the edge of the golf course itself. Now, keep to the well-waymarked and mown route, which curves through the golf course along the ridge. There are views of the Bristol Channel and beyond to your left. As you descend to the farthest edge of the golf course, pass an old stone barn to your right. From here descend to take a gate ahead in the boundary perimeter. Carry on ahead up a bank into a field. Cross

the field towards woodland ahead. Go through a gate, cross over a track and through another gate to continue on the path opposite. Go ahead over a stile and continue on the fenced path, with woodland alongside on your left and a field on your right. At the end of the field, cross a stile to enter the woodland. In the woodland follow the path near to the left-hand boundary until you go through a wooden gate ahead. From here the track becomes more distinct. Carry on through the woodland as the track gradually descends. When you exit the woodland continue on the hedged track downhill to reach a lane at Upper Canada.

H Turn left down the lane for about 100 metres and then take the minor road on the right. Follow the road uphill past a farm and several cottages. Continue on up the road, passing through scrubby woodland. Eventually you reach Gratton's Farm on the right. Soon you go through a gate to reach a T-junction of tracks. Turn left and uphill towards Christon Plantation (again). Follow the track down and round to the right with the woodland. You ignore a turn off to the left and follow the track within the edge of the woodland to reach the junction you passed through earlier in the walk. You now retrack your previous route all the way up to Keepers Cottage again.

I This time, do not turn right at Keepers Cottage. Instead continue ahead. Follow what soon becomes a metalled lane, down a wooded combe until you reach the edge of Christon and, shortly after, a junction with Banwell Road. Turn left along Banwell Road and after about 200 metres you reach the church. **A**

Rockhampton, Shepperdine and Hill

Distance 8.5 miles / 14 kms

Time 4 hours

OS Map Explorer 167

Starting Point The cricket ground, Lower Stone Road, Rockhampton - OS reference 653936

Parking Free parking at or on the grass verges in the vicinity of the cricket ground

Reaching the start from Bristol Go north on the M5. Leave by Junction 14. Turn left to go south on the A38 for 200 metres then take the lane off to the right signed for Rockhampton. Continue to Rockhampton and the cricket ground is off to the left

Refreshments None

THIS SCENIC and tranquil walk explores the vale along the Severn Estuary. It encompasses the attractive village of Rockhampton, sections along and across several rhynes, a length along the estuary from which there are extensive long distance views, and a traverse of agricultural fields and a country estate. This is a relatively flat walk taking in a combination of old tracks, minor lanes and footpaths. Some of the tracks can be muddy.

The route soon exits Rockhampton along an old green lane. It crosses several rhynes before following one to reach the hamlet of Shepperdine, with Oldbury Power Station visible ahead on the horizon. From Shepperdine the route proceeds directly, along a lane and then a track, towards the River Severn estuary. The stretch along the estuary is often bracing and always attractive. The walk returns inland via sluice gates and follows a further major rhyne towards and past Brickhouse Farm. From here you cross through fields and the grounds of Hill Court mansion, with the Cotswolds as a backdrop. Upon reaching the hamlet of Hill you take a further quiet lane/track/footpath route back towards Rockhampton.

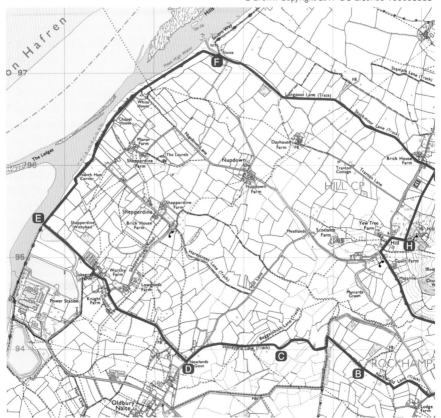

A With the cricket ground on your left walk westwards along the main village road passing several houses on the left. Shortly you come to a crossroads. Go ahead for about 50 metres and then take a waymarked track through a field gate, adjacent to a motor repair workshop. Proceed ahead on the track, Northfield Lane, which quickly becomes a hedged green lane. Stick with the green lane for about 700 metres, as it turns left and then sharply right, until you reach a field gate across it.

B Go through the field gate and bear slightly right to cross the open field towards a waymark post and gap by a tree. Keep towards the left hedge and proceed across the next field. Go through two successive gates in close proximity to cross a rhyne and enter a further field. Proceed towards the bridge you can see ahead. Take the gate to cross the bridge over a major rhyne. On the other side of the bridge, head up the bank and bear slightly left in the general direction of the far left-hand corner of the field – the path is not distinct. Soon you will see a gate ahead of you to aim for. Go through the gate and over

D Proceed along the lane for about 600 metres until the road bends around to the right. Here continue straight on down the no through road. First go past an equestrian complex on your left, and then take a right-hand fork in the track to pass a farmhouse immediately on your right. Continue past an extensive poultry farm complex on your right. Beyond the poultry farm and at the end of the surfaced road, look out for a field gate on your right. Take the stile immediately to its right, which is not immediately visible. Climb into the field and continue in the same direction as previously, now sticking with the left-hand boundary, which borders woodland. Continue through a field gate into a second field from which the embankment of the Severn Estuary now becomes clearly visible. Cross the field and go through another gate. Still keeping with the left-hand boundary, pass through a further field to reach a stile in the fence beneath the embankment.

E Cross the stile, climb the embankment and turn right to proceed along the estuary footpath. You follow this for the next 2000 metres or so. You go past the former Windbound Inn and through a gate, then past the converted Chapel House, the channel lights, the White House and a further gate. Keep on the embankment alongside the estuary and then follow the path as it swings round to the right to reach an inlet with sluice gates.

F Cross the sluice gates and turn right, away from the estuary, along a track, with the rhyne on your right. Proceed ahead through two gates in close succession. Now within a long field you proceed in the same direction, initially down the

another rhyne. Go ahead and along the left-hand boundary of the field. At the end of the field follow the track to enter another field. Bear left down the middle of this narrow field. At the end of the field, go through the gate.

C Turn right along a well-defined track, with a rhyne on the left and hedge on the right. Continue with this track, as Oldbury Power Station appears ahead of you on the horizon. Stay with the track until you reach a road. Turn left and proceed for about 150 metres, beyond a farm and other dwellings. Take the right hand turn signposted to Shepperdine.

centre of the field but eventually veering slightly left to pick up a gate ahead, which you go through. Then keep closely to the left-hand boundary as the field funnels off to the left. Follow the funnel to take the gate immediately ahead, leading straight onto a grassy track. Stick with this raised hedged green lane for about 1500 metres. A rhyne is alongside to the right for the whole of this distance, with a further rhyne alongside to the left for most of the way. You pass through two successive field gates on route. Eventually Brickhouse Farm appears on the horizon; before reaching it you go through a further field gate. Pass the farm on your left and cross the road ahead. From crossing the road, proceed ahead for 200 metres in the same direction until reaching a stile on your right.

G Cross the stile. You are now heading in the direction of Hill Court, with the Cotswolds rising on your left. Proceed straight ahead via field gates through the next two fields ahead. In the third field go straight ahead towards a visible stile ahead. Take the double-stiles to enter the grounds. Keeping on a straight line proceed to cross a metal stile and a grassy track. Take a line on a waymarked conifer in front of you and continue to follow waymarks through the parkland in parallel with the frontage of the house. Cross the private drive and go up an embankment to take a gate.

H You are now on the fenced main drive. Turn right down the drive and through a field gate to reach a road. Proceed along the road for about 150 metres until, just before a pillar box, you reach Woodend Lane on your left signed 'unsuitable for motor vehicles'. Take this metalled lane and continue past houses, a farm and further houses on your left. Continue with the lane as it morphs into a broad hedged track. Shortly after

passing the last houses you pass a foot-bridge and stile on the right. Do not take this footpath but note that from this point you need to keep with the hedged track for about a further 500 metres. Stay with it as it gradually curves round to the left. As soon as you see a small copse in the distance ahead of you, look out for two metal field gates in close succession on your left. Pass both of these, but within about 30 metres of the second one you will need to take an easily missed field gate set back in the hedge on the right.

1 When I last visited, the gate was in ramshackle condition and betrayed no clear indication of any footpath. However, a recently installed metal kissing-gate should be visible across the field. Enter the field and bear left across it in the direction of this gate. Go through the gate. In the next field, initially keep with right-hand boundary but then veer towards and through a field gate directly ahead. In the field beyond, keep to the left-hand boundary to pass through a further gate on to the main village road of Rockhampton. At the road turn right and you are very nearly back where you started. Immediately on your left you see the cricket ground and the starting point. **A**

Slimbridge and Frampton-on-Severn

Distance 7 miles / 11 kms

Time 3 to 3.5 hours

OS Map Explorer OL14

Starting Point St John's Church, St John's Road, Slimbridge - OS reference 740035

Parking Free parking in the village hall car park, on the road and opposite the church

Reaching the start from Bristol Go north on the M5. Leave by Junction 14. Go north up the A38 via Stone and continue until you reach the roundabout junction with the A4135. Here turn left and follow the main village road into Slimbridge

Refreshments The Three Horseshoes, Frampton-on-Severn

THIS WALK explores the wide flat expanses alongside the Severn Estuary; and in particular the vale between the villages of Slimbridge and Frampton-on-Severn. Much of the walk is along the Gloucester and Sharpness Canal. There are excellent views across the estuary towards the Forest of Dean and Wales; and plenty of opportunities to see wild birds. Frampton is an attractive village with plenty of historic interest. This walk is one of the easiest in the book, the terrain being very flat and the walking being mainly on well-defined tracks and paths.

From the start in Slimbridge the route soon passes through the churchyard of an interesting church. It then heads across countryside to briefly follow the banks of the River Cam before going through an extensive area of newly planted woodland to reach the outer fringes of Frampton. You initially skirt the western edge of the village, passing by several lakes created from disused gravel workings. You go on through parkland to skirt Frampton Court and then reach Frampton village green and its ponds. Exiting the village, the walk soon reaches the Gloucester and Sharpness Canal, which it follows south for a considerable distance providing the opportunity to observe canal craft as well as birdlife and panoramic views. From Cambridge Arms Bridge you briefly keep with a rhyne and then pass through an old orchard before retracing some of the outward route beyond the church and back to the start.

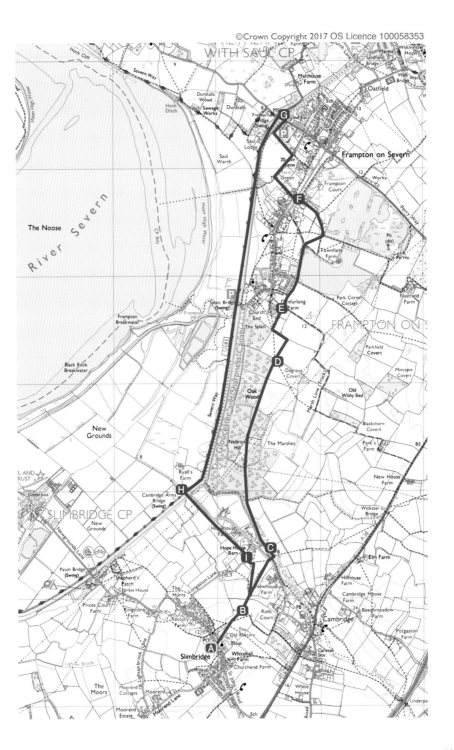

©Crown Copyright 2017 OS Licence 100058353

91

A The walk starts at the church opposite the public car park. Exit the car park and cross the road to enter the churchyard. Pick up the signed footpath and continue through the gate in the left-hand corner. Enter the field. Bear left across the field and through a gap. Continue straight along the full length of the next field, keeping with the left-hand boundary towards a stile ahead.

B Cross the stile and go straight along the fenced path. Go through a gate and continue with the path as it bends around to the right. Soon a stile appears off to your left. Take this to enter a field. Follow the path down the right-hand hedge of the field all the way to a stile in the right-hand corner. Take this to reach a lane. At the lane turn right and after about 50 metres go left up a track and through a gate. Follow the track over a bridge. Proceed ahead to the pumping station. Take a stile behind the building to enter a field.

C Proceed along the footpath with the river on your left through two fields. At the end of the second field, go over a concrete bridge ahead which crosses a tributary of the main river. After crossing the bridge immediately bear right and downhill. Follow the waymark sign to take the track entering woodland. From here onwards, you will be walking through woodland for at least 1500 metres. There is only one track; it is well waymarked and is also generally straight. Ignore all side tracks as you proceed. At a complex junction of tracks, head straight across on the waymarked footpath with electricity lines crossing diagonally ahead of you and with a cluster of three pylons over to your left. Pass beneath each of the parallel electricity lines. Keep with the waymarked track as it continues ahead and crosses another track to enter denser woodland. You eventually emerge on a surfaced crossing track, with a rhyne running immediately adjacent. Keep straight ahead to cross both the track and the rhyne. You are now skirting the right-hand edge of the woodland. In due course the track exits the woodland into an open field. Continue ahead in the same direction on the now surfaced track within the field, with the woodland now on your left, until reaching the field end coinciding with the furthest extent of the woodland.

D In the field ahead keep with the track straight ahead. Following the edge of the field, and as the track bends around to the left keep with it to reach a field gate in the corner. Frampton Church is now clearly visible off to your left but do not head in this direction. Instead your destination is to the right of the farm complex immediately ahead. From the gate turn sharp right for about 30 metres along the field boundary and then turn sharp left to pick up an indistinct path, which initially runs parallel with the continuation of the track you have just been on. As you near the farm over on the left, cross a track and then bear slightly left to follow the adjacent left-hand boundary of the field. You are aiming for a hidden stile towards the left-hand corner of the field boundary ahead.

E Go over the stile and the crossing surfaced track. Continue ahead along a wooded track, which skirts various houses on the left before reaching the gated end of a residential road. Take a stile to cross the road. Proceed straight ahead along the now narrow but still wooded path, passing between a small lake on the left and a much a larger one on the right: products of gravel workings. The path emerges via a stile into a field. Head for the gate immediately ahead of you, keeping to the edge of the lake on your right. Go through the gate into a boatyard. Continue ahead through the boatyard, passing to the left of the yachting clubhouse. Take a stile to cross the club driveway. Take the further stile immediately opposite to enter a field. Proceed diagonally right across the field to its far right-hand corner, keeping to the left of a clump of conifers ahead. Cross the stile and in the next field, detour to the right for about 50 metres to view a further lake. Then retrace your footsteps. Frampton Court is now visible ahead of you and its associated parkland is off to your right. Bear right towards a field gate. Go over the adjacent stile to pick up the residential lane ahead.

Continue with the lane to reach the village green of Frampton-on-Severn. Cross the green and the main road. Head towards the left-hand edge of a pond (although you may want to detour to the seat over to the right).

F Stick closely with the minor road that abuts the left-hand edge of the pond and go towards the line of houses ahead. If you want to detour for The Three Horse-shoes then turn left along the frontage – the pub is clearly visible. Otherwise look out immediately ahead for the signed footpath along a narrow lane between Roes Pool House and Cant Leaze/Pool Cottage. Take the lane and, after passing a Congregational Church on your right, continue on the hedged/ fenced path ahead as it passes out of the built up area. Go over a ditch and a stile into an open field. At the end of the field, go over a further stile on to a crossing track. Here turn right and follow the track ahead for about 200 metres to the right-hand corner of the field. At this point join a path coming in from the right. Turn left and very soon take the stile into a further field. In the field, keep to the right-hand boundary adjacent to a rhyne. Continue to the next field corner. Take a stile, turn right up the bank and then take a further stile to reach the Gloucester and Sharpness Canal towpath. Turn right and follow the towpath to reach Fretherne Bridge.

G Cross the bridge and turn left to pick up the towpath on the other side. For about the next 3,000 metres or so you simply follow this. On route you have glimpses of the Severn to your right and pass Frampton church, Splatt Bridge and

the edge of the woodland you traversed earlier to your left. The canal follows a generally straight path. As it bends slightly away to the right with a recently built dwelling over to the left, you reach Cambridge Arms Bridge.

H Leave the towpath and cross the bridge. Ahead and over to your right you will see an electricity sub-station. Turn right through a gate towards this and cross a concrete bridge over a rhyne. Here immediately take the two successive gates off to the left to follow a footpath running between the rhyne on your left and the sub-station on your right. Carry on with the path alongside the rhyne as it enters a field beyond the sub-station. At the left-hand corner of the field, go through a field gate to enter another field. In this field stick to the left-hand field boundary; firstly continuing alongside the rhyne and then with the hedge. Pass over a stile into a further field, which was obviously once an orchard. Keep to the left hand boundary and then go through a gate into a garden. From

here carefully follow the waymarks on a somewhat circuitous route. You end up on a fenced path between several residential properties, eventually emerging on to a lane.

I Cross the lane and take the stile immediately ahead into a field. In the large field, firstly bear right to pass the projecting corner of the next field and then head towards the stile in the far left-hand corner. You have now re-joined your outward route. Cross the stile and turn right to pick up the fenced path you took earlier. Retrace your steps through the gate to retake the stile you previously crossed. Upon re-entry into the field, the spire of Slimbridge church is clearly visible ahead. Continue across the field ahead, following a line just to the right of the church. Further retrace your footsteps through the gap in the field boundary and then across the stile in the churchyard wall. Pass again through the churchyard, across the road and back to the car park where you started. **A**

Dursley, Uley and Owlpen

Distance 8.5 miles / 14 kms

Time 4 to 4.5 hours

OS Map Explorer 167

Starting Point Long-stay car park, May Lane, Dursley - OS reference 754982

Parking May Lane free long-stay car park or other free long-stay parking in Dursley

Reaching the start from Bristol Go north on the M5. Leave by Junction 14. Go north up the A38 via Stone and continue. Turn right on the B4066 towards Dursley town centre. In the town centre turn right at the first roundabout to go into May Lane. The car park is off to the right about 100 metres along

Refreshments Old Crown, Uley; the New Inn, Old Spot Inn or other in Dursley

---

THIS VARIED WALK explores the Cotswold countryside to the east of the market town of Dursley. It includes plenty of ups and downs along the escarpment from Dursley, superb panoramic views, varied woodland, an interesting prehistoric fort and a long stretch alongside a small river. Walking is on paths, tracks and quiet lanes. There are a couple of muddy stretches.

The walk first passes through the historic centre of Dursley before exiting sharply uphill up and over Peaked Down, and then Cam Long Down. You climb again steeply up to the substantial Iron-Age fort at Uley Bury. After descending again through woodland to the village of Uley, the route follows a quiet lane to the secluded hamlet of Owlpen, passing by the Tudor manor-house. There then follows a long relatively flat stretch along the course of the River Ewelme. Eventually you deviate to climb up the side of the valley into Cooper's Wood. You follow the edge of the woodland and the escarpment back in the direction of Dursley with views back over towards Peaked Down and Cam Long Down. Upon returning to the edge of Dursley there is a final climb through Hermitage Wood with panoramic views across the town, before a final descent to the starting point in the centre.

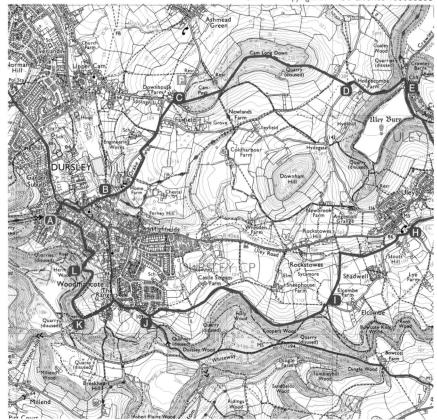

A From the car park go back down May Lane towards the town centre. At the roundabout turn right up the pedestrianised Parsonage Street in the direction of the Market House. Head left in front of the Market House and cross the road to pick up Long Street opposite. Proceed downhill on Long Street until you reach the Priory ahead. Where the main road curves round to the left, bear right and then continue straight ahead on a track. Ignore a path off to the right and continue straight ahead up a narrow path.

B Go through a gate and continue up the stepped path through woodland until you curve round to the right to reach another gate at the top. Go through this and exit the woodland. Follow the fenced footpath as it crosses two fields. At the end of the second field, you reach a stile in the left-hand corner. Continue on the still fenced path, following the right-hand boundary to exit on to a lane via a stile. Turn right on the lane and proceed gently uphill for about 350 metres until you reach a junction with Farfield, a lane off to the right. Here take the gate immediately ahead to enter a field. Follow the path to another gate in the hedge ahead. In the next field continue on the same line to a further

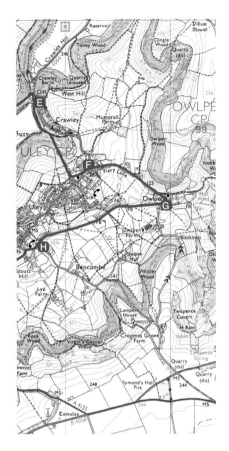

Initially go straight ahead for about 30 metres to a smaller waymark post, and from here take the left-hand fork uphill to enter scrubland. You continue to climb, emerging into open countryside before reaching the ridge of Cam Long Down, with extensive views on all sides. Continue along the full length of the ridge until you reach the waymark post at the end. From here, continue on the same footpath to descend steeply through woodland, following a winding path down to take a stile out of the woodland and into a field. In the field, continue to descend steeply in the direction of a stile at a hedge corner, following some further steps and a further waymark post. Cross the stile into another field. Keep to the left-hand edge before crossing a stile in the far corner on to a lane. Continue ahead on the hedged lane for about 150 metres to a T-junction.

D At the junction go left on the fenced/hedged track. Follow this track as it curves right and heads uphill, passing between Hodgecombe Farm and Springfield Farm. Keep with the track as it enters woodland and becomes increasingly sunken and steep. Persist uphill through the woodland all the way towards the main road, which becomes audible ahead. At the top, pass (or more likely rest at), a seat on the left and then go straight ahead through the exit gate to reach a parking area by the road. Before actually reaching the road, however, turn right through a gate to take another broad tree-lined track uphill.

gate, leading out on to a lane in front of Down House Farm. Turn right on the lane for about 50 metres until it curves left ahead. Here take the gate ahead.

C Take the path leading uphill through the trees. You soon take a left-hand fork up the steps. Cross the drive and another crossing path. Continue steeply uphill to the top of Peaked Down. After admiring the panoramic views, descend straight ahead in the direction of the trees ahead. Towards the bottom of the slope keep right to pick up a prominent waymark post. The waymark signs a multiplicity of paths – so be careful!

E After about 100 metres you emerge from the woodland to reach the edge of Uley Bury, an Iron-Age fort. Take the path off to the left, following the perimeter of the earthworks for about 200 metres before following a waymark post to fork off left, steeply down the earthworks and in the direction of woodland. Upon reaching the woodland enter via the gate immediately in front of you. Within the woodland continue straight ahead on the same path (ignoring all side paths). The path descends diagonally along the wood to eventually reach a gate, from which you emerge from the woodland into a field. Continue on the top edge of the field. Before reaching the corner, bear right and steeply down the field in the direction of Uley church ahead. At the bottom, go through the gate in the boundary. Continue along the enclosed footpath, turning left alongside the church wall, to pass the church and then emerge on to a road in the centre of Uley. Immediately cross the road and turn left.

F Almost immediately turn right in front of the Old Crown pub. Continue, initially downhill, along Fiery Lane, which is signposted to Owlpen, your next destination. Follow the undulating lane for at least 600 metres, ignoring all side paths and tracks on route, until you reach the signed entrance to the Tudor Owlpen Manor on your left. Do not take this. Instead take the right-hand stile opposite, adjacent to Marlings End. Head down the field, at first in the direction of the field gate at the bottom. As you near the field gate, however, take a stile ahead to enter a small copse. Go over a second stile and then a small bridge to the River Ewelme. Then imme-

diately take a further stile on your right to enter a field.

G Continue ahead in the field, following alongside the river on your right for a very considerable distance. Continue across four fields through a succession of gaps/gates/stiles. At the end of the fourth field, as it tapers towards the corner, cross a footbridge over a brook; and then head uphill and through a gate in a hedge. Continue up the next field and through a gate. In the final field, with the river still over to your right, you contour along the slope of a bank; before descending to take a gate in the far field corner on to an enclosed path. Follow the path ahead over a drive and through trees to reach a road at Stouts Hill.

H Turn right down the road. After about 100 metres take the first turn off to the left, signed to Elcombe. Continue with the lane as it bends right. Where it curves left, ignore the first public footpath sign but look out for a second one 50 metres further on, alongside Spring Mill, up a tree-lined track. Take the sunken track uphill. As the track levels out, it passes a recreation ground on the left and two houses on the right. Continue on in the same direction to reach the rear yard of the second house, Windsor House. Cross the yard to the stile straight ahead (ignoring the one off to the right). Continue ahead down the field and through a gate. In the next field proceed straight ahead (do not bear right) to take a stile in the far boundary, leading into a spinney. Turn left on a fenced path to reach a further stile and to enter a field. Follow the right-hand hedge until, about 50 metres beyond an electricity pole, you take a stile off to the right into another field. Bear left up this field to take a stile in the right-hand corner. In the next field continue uphill with the right-hand boundary, to cross a further stile on to a track.

I Turn right and proceed along the track for about 50 metres past Rowden House. Take a green lane going off to the left up into woodland. Climb steadily up the potentially muddy lane between steep wooded embankments for about 300 metres until you reach a diagonally crossing track. Here take the right-hand track going downhill through woodland. You soon reach the right-hand edge of the woodland, which you now stay near for a considerable distance. Continue along the now undulating track until you reach the point where it sharply turns back upon itself uphill. Here take the sunken path straight ahead, carrying on in the same direction as previously. The path proceeds gradually downhill, continuing to follow the edge of the woodland and curving to the left. The path emerges from the woodland but remains bounded by trees for a while yet. Soon you reach a crossing track, where you turn left. Continue downhill on the hedged path. Eventually the path levels out and evolves into more of a track as it passes various farm buildings and dwellings and climbs up to the A4135.

J At the road turn right. Head downhill into Dursley. Cross the road to reach the New Inn on the left. About 100 metres further on from here, look out on the left for the junction to Nunnery Lane. Take Nunnery Lane, following it as it curves round uphill past houses. Keep with the lane as it ascends beyond the built-up area and grows steeper – becoming hedged and impassable for vehicles. As you enter woodland, you reach a major crossing track.

K Turn right and persist with this gently undulating and meandering track as it contours the hillside, just within the edge of the woodland and with Dursley down to the right. Continue onwards until you reach a waymarked crossing of major paths.

L Here turn right and follow the narrow sunken path downhill. You shortly emerge from woodland. Continue downhill past two houses to join a lane. Within about 100 metres of joining Fort Lane, and just before the lane curves

away down to the right, look out for a public footpath sign off to the left. Turn left and follow an enclosed metalled path, which shortly curves right and continues downhill to a road. Turn left for about 100 metres along Upper Poole Road. Then turn right along the no-through road (Boulton Lane) via bollards to a T-junction. About 100 metres to your left is the Market House. Head towards this and then bear left down Parsonage Street. Re-join May Lane and turn left to return to the start. **A**

Dundry and Maes Knoll

Distance 8 miles / 13 kms

Time 4 hours

OS Map Explorer 154

Starting Point Dundry Down car park, Downs Road, Dundry - OS reference 556667

Parking Free car park

Reaching the start from Bristol Take the A38 south out of Bristol. Just after a petrol filling station on the left and opposite to Barrow Gurney reservoir on the right, look out for a left-hand turn signed to Dundry. Keep going uphill until you reach Dundry Inn in the village centre, at the top. Turn right and you soon reach the car park

Refreshments Dundry Inn, Dundry. There are several picnic seats with panoramic views in the vicinity of Norton Malreward

---

THIS WALK starts at the elevated village of Dundry, on the edge of Bristol, and incorporates spectacular views over the city, the Chew Valley and beyond to the south plus a notable Iron-Age hill fort. Much of the terrain is flat but there is a prolonged uphill climb towards the end of the walk. The route is mainly on tracks and paths. The early section out of Dundry can be muddy.

From Dundry the walk follows an elevated ridge with continuous views across Bristol. The route crosses the source of the Malago Brook, a tributary of the River Avon, which is culverted across much of the city. From here you climb gently towards and up to Maes Knoll, a hill fort built in around 250BC from which there are stunning panoramic views over a wide area. The walk descends to and through the village of Norton Malreward and continues via the Forest of Avon Community Forest Path to Norton Hawkfield and along the valley to North Wick. After this you climb at first steeply and then more gradually all the way back to Dundry in a roughly straight line, passing through various farms, fields and smallholdings on the way. The prominent Dundry telecom and church towers aid navigation back to the starting point.

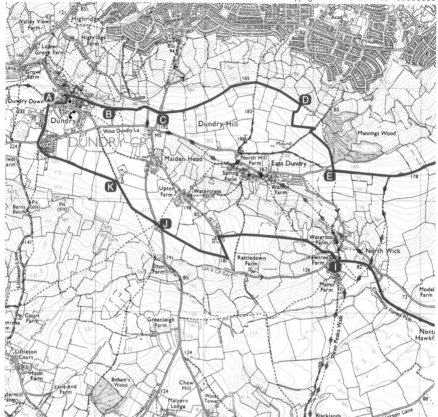

A From the car park, head back down the road towards the church. At the road junction turn left and, following the churchyard boundary, soon fork right along Hill Road. Continue with the metalled road until its end at a metal barrier.

B Cross the barrier to continue on a grass track. Within about 50 metres you reach a field gate and stile. Go over the stile and into a field. Go ahead towards the waymark post ahead. Follow the sunken track alongside the left-hand hedgerow to go through a gate in the corner. Proceed downhill with the hedge to your right to

take a metal gate at the bottom of the field. Go through a small copse to reach a lane. Go straight ahead on the surfaced lane for about 100 metres to reach a road.

C Cross the road and go straight ahead on the byway ahead, Middleway Lane. Proceed along the hedged track past Rosslyn on the right and through field gates until you eventually enter a field. Proceed on the now sunken track, with the hedge on your left, through another field gate. In the next field continue in the same direction, keeping alongside the hedge and passing an OS trig point. In the left-hand corner climb a stile. In

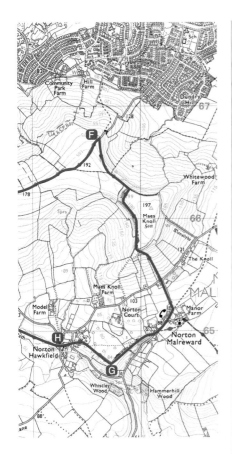

boundary into a second field via a gap. In this field continue with the left-hand boundary and take a stile ahead in the far boundary, leading on to a track. Cross the track and enter another field, indicated as land belonging to the Woodland Trust. Bear slightly right downhill on a grassy track towards woodland. You reach a junction with a track at the bottom of the valley. Turn right on this track alongside the Malago Brook. You shortly cross the brook. Beyond here, climb uphill, with the woodland on your right. Keep uphill on the grassy track, ignoring all turnings off to the left, until you eventually reach a stile. Go over the stile, turn right on a track and almost immediately through a field gate. Proceed beyond this gate for 20 metres and then take a stile on your left into a field. Go down the field keeping to the left-hand hedge to reach a stile out on to a lane.

E Turn left on the lane. You need to stick with this lane for about 1500 metres. You climb uphill gradually, with panoramic views appearing on both the left and right. You reach the brow of the hill and begin to descend. About 300 metres beyond the brow look out for a signed footpath on the right, next to a tree. Go through the gate to take this footpath. Keep towards the right-hand boundary and gradually climb the field towards a gate in far top corner. Go through the gate and turn left, taking the left-hand boundary and heading towards the obvious ramparts of Maes Knoll. Ascend the ramparts and turn right to follow them. When you reach the corner of the ramparts, curve left and downhill to traverse the full length of the fort, along its perimeter. At the far

the next field immediately take the right-hand stile to enter a further field. Cross this field to take a stile in the far hedge. In the following field, continue ahead in the same direction towards the hedged corner. At the corner pick up and follow the right-hand hedge all the way to the end of the field. Do not take the field gate directly ahead of you.

D Take the stile in the corner on your right. In the next field proceed uphill, with the boundary to your left. As you near the top of the field look out for a stile on your left. Take this and then go down the field, following the left-hand

end of the fort, head towards a gate in the right-hand corner.

F Go through the gate. Turn right, keep with the right-hand hedge and go through a gap in the boundary. In the next field, beyond a mound on your left, follow the grassy track for a short distance as it curves leftwards and downhill. Then take the gate in the hedge off to the left into a further field. Keep downhill with the track as it follows the right-hand hedge. As it curves to the right you may wish to make a short detour to the well-positioned seat ahead, with views down to the village of Norton Malreward. Continue downhill with the right-hand boundary, through a field gate and down the field. Keep with the right-hand boundary all the way, to exit a gate on to the road. Turn left on the road and then almost immediately turn

right on to another road signed to Stanton Drew. Pass through the village of Norton Malreward on this road. Continue as the road curves round to the right. Go beyond Chalk Farm Close.

G Just before the road bends to the left, take a wooden gate on the right between trees. With a stream initially down to your left, walk along the path for about 100 metres until you take a metal gate on the left into a field. Head uphill through trees to take another gate in the right-hand corner. Continue on the waymarked path, following it as it bends right around the field corner. There are several seats in this vicinity. From the corner head towards the obvious farm complex ahead. Proceed through a field gate into Park Farm. Go ahead into the farmyard and follow the waymarks directing you left between the barns to

and through a gate and on to a lane. At the lane go left and immediately right down another lane. Follow the lane downhill and upon reaching a small triangle of open land take the left track down to a further lane. Cross this lane and take a gate into a field.

H In the field, follow the left-hand boundary for about 50 metres until you go through another gate on the left to enter a copse. Turn right and soon follow a well-defined hedge to your right, with a stream away to your left. Cross the stream via a footbridge to exit the copse and enter a field. In the field proceed to the right-hand corner and across another footbridge. In the next field go sharp right for about 50 metres to take a gate. Go through the following field, with the stream on your right, and take consecutive gates in the hedge. In the further

field follow the stream on your right for about 100 metres and then take a footbridge on your right into another field. Bear half-left across this field to take a gate. Continue across the next field towards another gate, to the left of a group of cottages ahead. Exit the gate on to a lane. Turn left and up the lane for about 250 metres until you reach a footpath sign off to the right between Yewtree Farm House and Yew Tree Barn.

I You take this footpath and in doing so soon cross two stiles. Follow the obvious path downhill with the right-hand boundary until a footbridge appears ahead. Cross the footbridge into the next field. Here bear left and steeply uphill to take a gate in the left-hand corner. In the next field continue to bear left steeply uphill to take a metal gate next to a tree. You immediately cross a bridge into a further field. Here turn left and keep with the left-hand field boundary for about 100 metres until reaching a field corner. At this corner look ahead uphill and half-right to identify the field gate you need to aim for. Proceed steeply uphill towards it. At the field gate there are views of Chew Magna Lake and a prominent farmhouse over to the left. Keep these to your left and continue straight ahead up the field, in the direction of buildings (of a smallholding) on the distant horizon and more immediately a gate in the field boundary ahead. Go through consecutive gates into the next field. Here keep towards the right-hand boundary and eventually go through the smallholding, emerging on to a road. At the road turn left for about 150 metres until you reach a footpath sign off to the right.

J Here go through the gate and bear right towards and through the field gate opposite. Now continue up the field hedge right to take a gate on the horizon. In the next field, keep the boundary to the right to take another gate. Continue on the same alignment across a further field. With a telecom tower now becoming increasingly prominent on the horizon, you exit via a field gate in the far corner on to a road. Cross the road and go right, before almost immediately picking up the footpath over to the left. Take a gate into a field and keep to the right-hand boundary, now heading in the direction of the telecom tower. As you enter a second field stick very closely with the right-hand hedge to reach the top right-hand corner. Here go through the gate and cross the field towards the left edge of the telecom tower compound.

At the compound go through a narrow gap between the hedge and the fence immediately to its left.

K Proceed down the short ginnel and through the gate at the end. Cross the driveway ahead and take another gate to enter a field. With Dundry church now prominent in the distance ahead, take the path off to the left, keeping the hedge/wall to your left. At the end of the first field, go through a gap to enter another. Continue in the same direction to take successive metal field gates ahead into a further field. Here, keep to the right-hand boundary, aiming towards the right-hand corner and a further field gate. Take the gate on to a track, which you follow between various houses to reach a road. You are now back in the village of Dundry. On the road, turn right and then immediately left into Downs Road. With the church tower increasingly evident, proceed for about 300 metres, passing various, mainly industrial, buildings before eventually returning to the car park and the start. **A**

Brockweir, Hewelsfield and St Briavels

Distance 8 miles / 13 kms

Time 4.5 hours

OS Map Explorer OL 14

Starting Point Hewelsfield Road, eastern edge of Brockweir - OS reference 542013

Parking Free on-road parking along a grass verge or elsewhere near the village edge on Hewelsfield Road, Brockweir

Reaching the start from Bristol Go west on the M4. Take the M48 and leave from Junction 2. Take the A466 for Tintern. Continue through Tintern for about a mile then turn right over the bridge to Brockweir. Continue uphill through Brockweir on the Hewelsfield Road until you reach the far edge of the built-up area

Refreshments The George Inn, St Briavels or the Brockweir Inn, Brockweir

---

THIS WALK explores the spectacular winding river and steep wooded cliffs of the Wye Valley, on the border between England and Wales. As well as the views of the gorge and towards the Forest of Dean, the walk incorporates the historic interest of St Briavels Castle, Hewelsfield Church and a long section on the 8th-century Offa's Dyke. This is a relatively challenging walk, including one stiff ascent. The walking is mainly on woodland and field paths.

From Brockweir, the walk gradually climbs alongside a stream and further uphill through woodland to the village of Hewelsfield, passing the unusual church, which is of Saxon origin. You continue along an enclosed wooded track and through a series of fields to St Briavels, with distant views to the Forest of Dean. St Briavels was the historic administrative centre of the Forest of Dean; its 13th-century castle was a combination of border stronghold, royal hunting lodge, prison and court. There follows a prolonged descent towards the River Wye. Just before Bigsweir Bridge the route diverts on the Offa's Dyke path and climbs steeply through fields and woodland with extensive views to the valley below. You then descend steeply along and down the wooded valley to rejoin the River Wye. You conclude with a gentle walk beside the river, all the way back to Brockweir Bridge, from where it is a short climb back to the start.

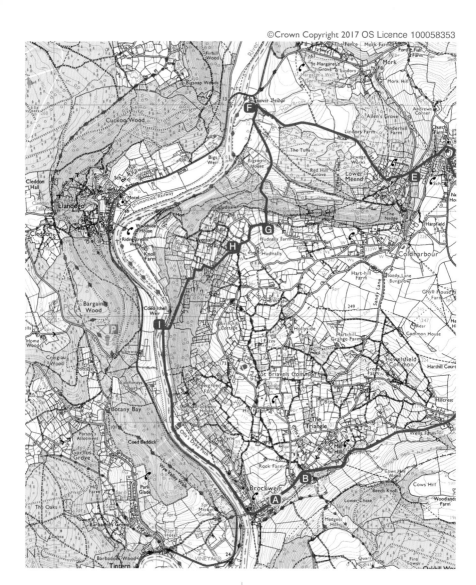

A The walk starts on the Hewelsfield Road at the edge of the built-up area of Brockweir. Take the footpath on the grass verge running alongside the road uphill in the direction of Hewelsfield. Pass a road turning to Coldharbour off to the left and a signed footpath off to the right before approaching the village hall (MacKenzie Hall).

B Immediately before the village hall take the track on its right immediately abutting its car park. The broad wooded track initially climbs but soon descends past several houses on the left and towards a stream on the right. Continue on this still wooded track alongside the stream, past a pond on the right and a further house on the left. You continue

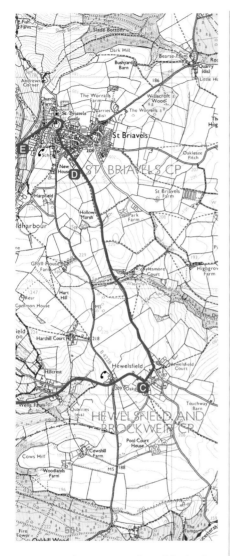

from the left. Continue further uphill on this wooded road, passing several houses before reaching a crossroads with the B4228, Chepstow to Coleford road. Keep straight ahead at the crossroads along Church Road towards the village of Hewelsfield and the interesting church of St Mary Magdalen.

C At the church, bear left with Church Road. After about a further 50 metres bear left to take a lane serving several houses. As the lane turns sharply to the right, go through a gate off to the left to take a track, passing in front of The Barn: Hewelsfield Court. Continue ahead up a fenced/ hedged track, which soon becomes sunken and more wooded. Climb a stone stile to enter a field. Keep to the left of a field and take a wooden stile ahead (ignoring a field gate in the corner) to enter a copse. Walk down a path through the copse. At the end, climb a stile and proceed on a hedged track. Pass to the left of a farm. Cross the farm drive to take a broad fenced track ahead. Cross a stile and, about 20 metres further on, another one taking you into a field. From here you proceed in a straight line and generally uphill, following the right hand boundary over successive stiles and through five fields. At the far end of the second field there are two ponds on the right. In the fourth field you pass a house on the right. In the fifth field, immediately after the second house turn right over a stile in the hedge on to a lane. You have now reached St Briavels; and there should be distant views of the Forest of Dean ahead of you.

past a sign 'to Spring Vale only'. As the track curves left to form the driveway to Spring Vale, continue straight ahead uphill on a tree-lined/ fenced path. The path climbs steadily, morphing into a track before reaching a lane. Turn right on the lane (Bailey Lane). Continue steeply uphill in the same direction until the lane merges with a road coming in

D Turn left and along the lane until you reach a crossroads. Cross straight over the B4228 (for a second time) to pick up Barrowell Lane, beyond a wooden barrier. After about 50 metres, turn right down Pystols Lane, passing Crown House (formerly the Crown Inn) on the right. Continue downhill, ultimately keeping ahead along a narrow walled path to reach a road in front of St Briavels Castle. Turn right on the road, and soon go ahead on a track, to start an anti-clockwise circuit of the outer perimeter of the castle. You pass The George public house off to your right and continue the circuit on the road. Upon completing about three-quarters of the circuit, you reach a viewing area with seats and picnic tables on your right. Just beyond here is a prominent waymark sign. Take the footpath down the sunken track. You soon reach a further road, where you turn left. You then see a signpost to Lower Meend. Proceed downhill in this direction, ignoring the minor road off to the left. You reach a complex junction of roads, where you first turn left, ignoring the road doubling back uphill, and then continue with the bend round to the right and downhill.

E Just beyond the bend on the left is a byway sign. Take the narrow hedged and sunken footpath downhill. Soon the path diverges by a small brick building on the left. You ignore the waymarked option straight ahead, instead taking the route jinking to the right and then left down a few steps. Continue steeply downhill, down further steps and between various houses and other buildings to reach a lane by Cherry Tree

Cottage. Turn right down this steep narrow lane through the cottages of Lower Meend. Ignore a turn to the right. Carry on downhill to enter woodland. About 50 metres before reaching the gates of a sewage works, turn left and take a stile. Immediately cross the stream and exit the woodland into a field. In the field turn right and walk downhill, following the right-hand boundary to go through a farm gate. Pick up the hedged farm track, soon passing Lindors Farm on your left. You continue to follow this sweeping broad track for a considerable way. It initially undulates before descending gradually, going through a succession of field gates and passing a bungalow on the left. At around the point that Bigsweir Bridge, (the road bridge across the River Wye), comes into view on your horizon, the track crosses a stream.

F Go over the stream. Immediately turn left and left again to take the wide track under an avenue of oak trees. Proceed

along this track for about 200 metres, re-crossing the same stream and another, before taking the Offa's Dyke Path waymarked off to the left. Proceed on the track up a field, beneath the power line and keep just to the right of an electricity pole. Go through a metal field gate into a large field. From the gate, bear right and uphill, aiming for a gap in the hedgerow about 50 metres to the right of the field gate in the highest corner of the field. On passing through the gap, do not be misled by the careless waymarking currently evident. To continue on the Offa's Dyke you must bear slightly right up the slope towards the woodland ahead and a field gate into it. Take the gate to enter the woodland. Follow the path as it goes steeply upwards. The route of the path is initially very clear but further up the hillside, as you clamber over moss-covered rocks, look out carefully for the yellow waymarks. Eventually these direct you to a prominent set of wooden steps with a handrail. Climb

these steps to reach a T-junction of paths. Turn right and then, within 50 metres, left. You follow the Offa's Dyke signs, up along a narrow walled path to emerge on a road, opposite to Birchfield House.

G Turn right at the road and proceed on the flat. Ignore a fork off to the right; instead keep with the road as it bears left and uphill. Take the first turn off to the right along a lane, with the Offa's Dyke signs. Follow the lane round to the left with a house on the right. Continue uphill on the hedged lane until you reach a waymarked fork.

H At this point, you leave the Offa's Dyke path, taking the right hand path to descend towards the gates of a house, Meg's Folly. Here keep with the track as it further descends into woodland. Keep on the walled track. Do not take the first path off to the right nor the second, left-hand path. However, about 50 metres

beyond the left-hand path, do take the narrow path off to the right. Continue down this path, between two low moss-covered walls and with a field over to your right, to reach a stone stile ahead. Do not take this. Instead take the path off to the left, continuing to follow a wall on the right and descending gradually through the woodland. You eventually cross over another path just beyond a cottage over to your right. Continue to descend from here on the same path and in the same direction for at least another 500 metres along and down the side of the valley. The River Wye gradually comes more into view and earshot. After the path passes over a small plank bridge, it curves rightwards and more steeply downhill through a gate to link up with the riverside path.

1 Turn left on the riverside path. You continue with the river on your right for about 2000 metres, passing a boathouse to the right and paddocks to the left. You go through several gates and stiles, and over a couple of wooden bridges on route. As Brockweir Bridge comes fully into view, continue along the hedged riverside path. As you near the bridge, the path becomes a lane along the old quayside. At the bridge, pick up the main road and turn left into the village. Pass the Brockweir Inn on your right and continue back up the Hewelsfield Road towards the start. **A**

Marshfield and Solsbury Hill

Distance 11 miles / 18 kms

Time 6 hours

OS Map Explorer 155

Starting Point Eastern end of High Street, Marshfield - OS reference 780737

Parking Plenty of free on-street parking in or just off the High Street

Reaching the start from Bristol Go east on the M4. Leave by Junction 18 and then go south on the A46. At the A420 roundabout turn left and proceed for two miles until you reach Marshfield, which is off to the right

Refreshments Plenty in Marshfield but none on route

THIS WALK samples some of the most striking scenery in the southern Cotswolds, including Solsbury Hill, the plateau of Charmy Down and lengthy stretches along St Catherine's Brook. It also features the historic village of Marshfield and skirts the Ashwicke Estate. This is a strenuous and undulating walk with a couple of steep climbs but it is well worth the effort. The route is mainly on well-defined tracks and paths – there are a couple of muddy stretches though.

The first section comprises a descent from Marshfield in the direction of Cold Ashton, following the attractive valley of St Catherine's Brook. You eventually leave the valley, climbing to the plateau of Charmy Down, a disued World War Two airfield and radar station. Beyond here the walk begins to skirt the built-up area of the city of Bath. After a steep descent into the combe of Chilcombe Bottom, there is an equally steep climb to the top of Solsbury Hill – but rewarded by the spectacular views of Bath. From Solsbury Hill the route gradually descends again through woodlands and fields to rejoin St Catherine's Brook. The route keeps with the brook again for some distance before diverting on another steep climb through fields and woodland towards the hamlet and country estate of Ashwicke. From here you climb steadily back towards Marshfield, a full length vista of which appears on the skyline ahead well before you reach it.

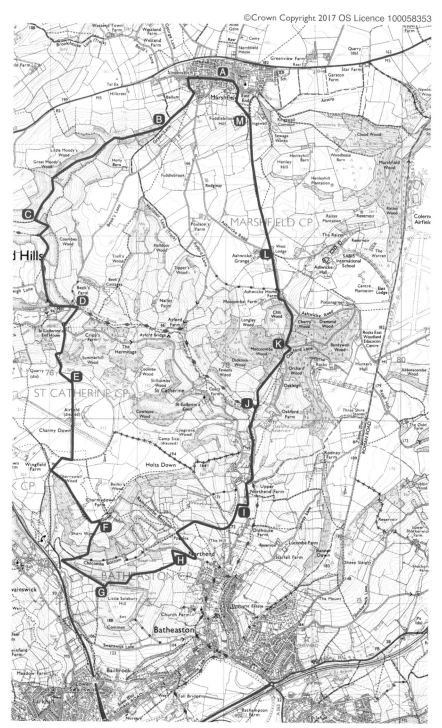

A The walk starts at the eastern end of Marshfield High Street, in the vicinity of the church. Head back down the High Street, away from the church for about 250 metres. Look out for St Martin's Lane on your left. Take this and proceed for about 200 metres until you reach a footpath on your right, signed to Cold Ashton. Go through the gate and bear left down to the left-hand corner of the field. Go through the gate into another field. Go straight ahead to cross a stile and enter the woodland ahead. Proceed on the track and look out for a further stile on your right within about 100 metres.

B Cross the stile and follow the path as it gradually descends down the valley side. Proceed along the valley floor with a small brook on your right for about 200 metres until a gate appears ahead of you to the right of the brook. Cross the brook over a concrete bridge and go through the gate ahead. Continue alongside the brook, now on your left, until passing through a further gate. Continue in the same direction but head very gradually up and away from the brook along the next field, following the contours of the hillside to reach a gap in the hedge. Continue in the same direction in the next field. At a junction of paths take the left lower fork. With derelict farm buildings up to your right, cross a stile and bear right uphill to the corner of the next field. Here take the footpath off to the left, keeping close to the boundary hedge on your left. Follow this path for about 300 metres as it undulates and becomes more defined. Look out for an obvious manhole cover on your left. About a further 50 metres beyond this, take a left-hand turn going down to a gate.

C Go through the gate into a field. Head straight downhill, eventually picking up a hedge as your right-hand boundary. Cross a stone footbridge and then immediately bear right up the hillside to take a gate into a field. Climb a couple of steps into the field before turning immediately left. Follow a well-defined footpath as it curves around the edge of the hillside until you reach a stile by a gate in the right-hand corner. Cross the stile and head downhill on the track, between the hedge on the left and an embankment on the right. Continue with the track as it undulates. The track reaches a stile by a field gate. Cross this and continue steeply uphill on the track until you join a lane. Proceed down the lane for about 30 metres to reach a footpath off to the left. Cross the stile and head down the track and field towards the house ahead, keeping towards the right-hand boundary. At the bottom, go through the gate to cross the driveway and a further gate to enter the field in front of the house. Continue along the field for about 50 metres.

D Here take the right-hand turn to cross a footbridge. Head uphill towards the far left-hand corner of the field where you go through a gate to reach a road next to a house. Turn left on the road for about 50 metres. Take the track ahead, go through the field gate and climb the steps to take the footpath off to the left via a spinney. At the top of the bank go through the gate into a field. Climb the field, keeping with the left-hand boundary. Ignore a small gate off to the left and continue further up the field beyond this to take a field gate. Follow the grassy track uphill, initially within woodland

and then with the boundary to your right. Go through a further gate and immediately bear left, passing a mound to your right, towards a soon visible gate in a fence ahead.

E Go through the gate into the old Charmy Down airfield. Pick up the track ahead and continue in a straight line, keeping an area of woodland to your right, before taking a field gate. In the next field proceed with the right-hand boundary to reach the far right-hand corner, where you bend right to exit with the track. Follow the track as it bends left through a field gate, past barns on the right and through a further field gate to reach a lane. Turn left at the lane and stick with this for about 600 metres, initially with woodland on your right. As you pass Cherrywell House on your left, views of the built up area of Bath start to appear on your right. After the lane curves round to the left, with woodland

now on your left, look out for a footpath sign on the right.

F Take the gate and head diagonally down the field towards the telegraph poles and then follow their alignment. Follow the waymarks on consecutive telegraph poles, and then on trees, to exit the field via scrubland, just to the left of their alignment. Keep to the left down the next field, going through a gap in the hedge and then down towards a further telegraph pole. Next to this is a stile. Cross the stile and follow the path down a long flight of steps through woodland. Tread carefully, especially in wet conditions. Eventually you reach a stile at the bottom. Take this and a few further steps down into a field. Here bear right downhill in the direction of derelict farm buildings, which may not initially be obvious. Go through the field gate to the right of the derelict buildings and then climb uphill in the same direction, pass-

ing just to the left of the trees ahead towards a gate in the hedge at the top of the field. Go through the gate to reach a grass verge. Turn left up the verge and proceed through a gate ahead. Make the short, steep ascent up Solsbury Hill, going through a further gate to reach a waymark post at the perimeter of the fort.

G At this point you are free to go to the top of Solsbury Hill and explore it more fully. Having done so, return to the way-mark post. From here (facing downhill towards the entry gate) turn right and follow the signed footpath sign for about 50 metres. Then look out for a gap in the scrub off to your left. Take the stepped path down through this scrub for about a further 50 metres to take a stile in the right-hand corner to enter woodland. Follow the path carefully as it curves left and right through the wood-land, eventually emerging via a stile into

a field. Proceed along the left-hand boundary of the field before taking a gate into the left-hand corner to enter a spinney. Continue in the same direction in the spinney, now with the boundary to your right. At the end of the spinney, go through the gap in the hedge into the next field. Bear left downhill towards a prominent footpath waymark in the left-hand corner of the field. At the way-mark, turn left to take a track. Walk down the next field with the hedge on your right. Stay with the track as it bends rightwards and pass through a gate. Keep with the now hedged track and soon reach a lane.

H Turn right on the lane downhill for about 200 metres until you see a foot-path off to the left. Go through the gate and downhill on the alignment of a house on the opposite hillside. At the bottom of the field cross the footbridge to enter another field. Here do not go

straight ahead but instead turn sharp right. Take a gate into a further field and head up towards the left-hand corner. Exit the field via a gate on to a lane. Turn right on the lane proceeding uphill past a group of houses to a junction. Here continue to follow Ramscombe Lane for about 200 metres until you see a footpath off to the right. Climb the stile into a field. Go downhill, keeping to the right of the house ahead to exit via stile on to a lane.

I Turn left along the lane and continue as it turns right, signed for Marshfield. You soon pass a water treatment works on your left. Cross the river and then immediately take the stile on your left. Walk the length of the meadow ahead, keeping the river to your left. Cross a stile next to a field gate, the drive ahead and another stile. Continue on the path as it merges into a driveway. When you reach a junction of driveways, cross the stile immediately ahead of you into a field. Continue on the path, following the stream on your left until you reach a footbridge

off to the left. Cross this and proceed on the flat until you reach a waymark by a group of trees. The ground conditions are often difficult here, so you may be forced to deviate slightly from the route indicated. Eventually you need to aim for a visible stile in the hedge at the top of the slope on your right. Proceed uphill towards this and cross a track, which runs alongside the hedge, to reach it.

J Cross the stile into a field. Bear right across the field towards the stile and sign ahead, with a large house away to your right. Pass the sign to enter the next field. Bear right across the field and eventually pick up the right-hand boundary. Exit via a stile in the corner. In the next field, continue downhill to pick up the right-hand boundary and, after passing a lake on your right, exit via a stile. Then exit out on to the road via a further stile. Turn left on the road for about 100 metres to take a footpath off to the left, signed to Ashwicke, via a green field gate.

K Proceed for about 50 metres along the track into woodland. Take the footpath up to the right via steps and a gate into a field. Climb the steep slope, keeping to the right-hand boundary. Continue on ahead through a gate. Then keep towards the left-hand boundary, gradually climbing the hillside, as the grassy track eventually reaches a gate giving access to a road. Turn left at the road and stay with it as it swings right, round Ashwicke Home Farm. Carry on for about 200 metres, with glimpses of Ashwicke Hall visible to the right, as the road enters woodland and soon after takes a sharp left-hand bend. Here take the signed footpath and gate straight ahead.

L Enter the field and keep to the right-hand boundary, go through a pair of gates either side of a track and continue in the same direction through another gate. Then continue in the same direction on a well-defined path across a field and through a further gate. In the next field keep the hedge to your left and proceed increasingly uphill until at the crest Marshfield comes into view. Descend gently towards the gate in the left-hand corner. In the next field continue in the same direction, hedge left, to reach the boundary corner. Go through the gate and keep on down, now with the hedge on your right, to another gate. Continue on the track in the direction of the church tower ahead, now keeping towards the left-hand hedge and climbing back uphill. Continue until shortly before reaching a further field gate. Do not go through this gate.

M Instead deviate left and uphill for about 50 metres towards another gate. Go through this into another field. The full length of Marshfield is now visible on the skyline. Follow the path downhill into a small valley. At the bottom, go through a gate and in the next field climb steeply uphill following the right-hand hedge. Go through the gate in the corner and climb the path between the houses to reach the road. At the road turn left. The road soon curves right, emerging into the east end of Marshfield High Street. **A**

Winscombe, Shipham and Dolebury

Distance 10.5 miles / 17 kms
Time 5.5 hours
OS Map Explorer 141
Starting Point King's Wood National Trust car park, Winscombe Hill, off the A38 near Sidcot - OS reference 422560
Parking Free parking at King's Wood car park
Reaching the start from Bristol Take the A38 south out of Bristol and beyond the Airport and Churchill. About a mile beyond the centre of Sidcot, over the brow of a hill and immediately after a filling station look out for a turning off to the right. Take the lane and the car park is immediately visible off to the left
Refreshments Lillypool Cheese and Cider café. Short signed detours to Lyncombe Lodge Hotel or facilities in Winscombe. Seats with good views later in the walk

---

THIS IS A CLASSIC Mendip walk incorporating some of the best open heathland, woodland, nature reserves, archaeology and panoramic views. It is strenuous, including a couple of steep climbs, but mainly follows well-maintained tracks.

The walk starts in King's Wood, from which you climb steeply on the ancient Winscombe Drove. After a brief descent you climb again gradually up the slope of Long Bottom to traverse, the mainly coniferous, woodland of Rowberrow Bottom. Upon exiting into open land you climb up on to the plateau of Black Down, the highest point of the Mendips, with spectacular views in all directions. Black Down is designated as being of both national scientific and archaeological significance; the latter on account of Bronze-Age tumuli and its use for decoy purposes in World War Two. The walk briefly descends into Rowberrow Warren again before emerging into the nationally important grassland/heathland of Dolebury Warren. There follows a further climb to the Iron-Age fort with spectacular views. After a brief descent to cross the A38 on the edge of Churchill, you climb Lyncombe Hill and follow Lyncombe Lane along a ridge through deciduous woodland, almost as far as Sandford. Here you descend to pick up the Strawberry Line, now a cycle path, through Winscombe until branching off via Sladers Leigh nature reserve to return to the start.

A Exit the car park, cross Winscombe Hill and take the footpath immediately opposite, leading you via woodland back towards the A38. When you reach the A38, turn left and proceed for about 50 metres to the brow of the hill. Cross the A38 via the second traffic island towards the start of a track signposted to Shipham. Proceed uphill through woodland on the metalled track, passing Rose Wood Cottage on the right. At a junction, just before a gate and wall, take the left fork. You are now on Winscombe Drove, which you will stick with for at least 1500 metres. Initially keep with the right-hand wall. Continue with the track as it wends its way upwards through trees. In due course the track emerges from the trees and narrows between hedges before broadening out again. Ignore a track off to the left, a crossing footpath and a second track off to the left. Continue on uphill in the same direction past Drove Farm buildings. After passing over the brow of the hill, descend towards a crossroads. Lillypool Cheese and Cider Farm, which also has a shop and café, is ahead on the right.

B Head straight across the crossroads, keeping the shop/café on your right (unless you wish to detour), to pick up the metalled lane straight ahead. Continue up the lane for about 1000 metres, climbing gradually and passing intermittent dwellings. Eventually you reach Longbottom Farm on the left. Just beyond here, as the road bends sharply round to the right and a footpath joins from the left, go straight ahead through the green metal barrier to pick up a track and to enter woodland and Rowberrow Warren. The track initially continues to head uphill in the same direction, before bending sharply left and downhill and then even more sharply right and uphill to join a junction of tracks.

C At the multi-track junction take the right-hand track. This track continues uphill, until very soon emerging from the woodland and Rowberrow Warren. Keep ahead on the fenced path between open fields, towards Tyning's Farm ahead. Keep with the track as it climbs through the farmyard and past the main farm buildings to reach a crossing track.

D Turn left on the track past the end of the farm buildings. Go uphill on the fenced path and through a gate at the top to enter the open moorland of Black Down. Proceed straight ahead on the wide moorland track, from which there are often magnificent views, particularly on a clear day. Stick closely to this track as it crosses others. Stay with the track as it curves round to the left; as soon as it begins to go downhill steeply, take a left-hand fork on a lesser path. Proceed gradually downhill on this well-defined path through bracken and past scattered holly and hawthorn trees in the general direction of a large expanse of woodland ahead. Continue downhill towards the woodland until you reach a T-junction. Here turn right and continue for at least 100 metres until you see a gate down to your left. Take the path leading this way and go through the gate to re-enter the woods of Rowberrow Warren. Go over the stream and over the crossing track. Within about 20 metres of the crossing track, take the minor path forking off to the right. Continue straight downhill on this narrow path through scrubby wood-

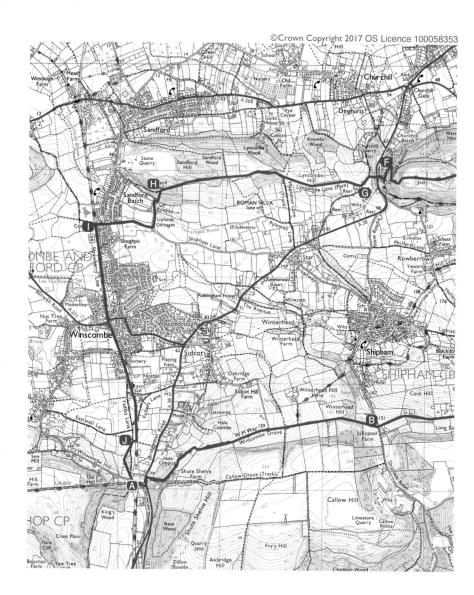

©Crown Copyright 2017 OS Licence 100058353

land until you reach a junction with a broader path. Here turn right, continuing downhill until you reach a divergence of paths. Here bear right and ahead into denser woodland. Keep straight ahead on this same path for about 100 metres, being very careful to ignore several deviations off to both the left and right. The path becomes walled. Soon a very obvious stile and gate appear on your left.

E Take the stile to exit Rowberrow Warren and enter the grassland of Dolebury Warren. Follow the left hand track uphill. Proceed over a stile next to a gate

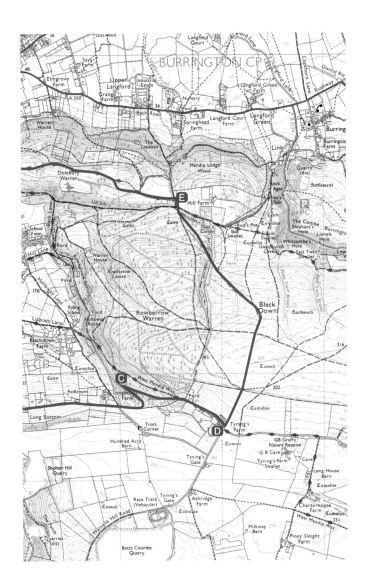

and carry on uphill until you reach a fork ahead of woodland. Here bear right and then left through the woodland, and then further uphill through a gate. Keep straight ahead uphill on the same track to traverse the ramparts of Dolebury Fort. Walk straight through the fort, initially bearing left and downhill with the main

track and then heading for a distinct gap in the far ramparts on the other side, with woods beyond. After passing through the gap, descend via the woodland on a stony track, which initially curves left and then bends back rightwards to a wooden gate. Exit the woodland and Dolebury Warren via the gate. Continue downhill for about

50 metres passing some houses on the edge of Churchill.

F At the T-junction ahead, turn left and go down a lane. At another T-junction turn right on another lane. Immediately you will see a telegraph pole with a left pointing footpath sign upon it, about 50 metres ahead of you. Turn left to take the narrow enclosed footpath, which climbs steeply up steps to the A38. Turn left for about 30 metres and cross the A38 to pick up the clearly visible footpath opposite. Go ahead steadily uphill for about 30 metres before bearing sharply to the left to take the obvious steep route uphill. At the top of this steep climb take the fenced path immediately ahead of you. At the end of this path, you reach a T-junction with a track. Turn left on the track. Within about 100 metres a wooden farm building appears on your right next to a junction.

G Take the right-hand turn on to Lyncombe Lane, which you will now stick with along the escarpment for at least 1500 metres. Keep with the hedged lane as it goes up and down, narrows and broadens and passes in and out of woodland – ignoring all side tracks and paths, left and right. After you pass over a crossing path, with the right-hand turn signposted off to Lyncombe Lodge Hotel, the lane begins to climb more steeply. You shortly go through a metal gate to enter a field. Keep with the track through a wooden gate and into a further field, in which the views of the valley to the left briefly open up. Keep ahead to take a metal field gate and re-enter woodland. You soon pass a quarry on the right. In due course the track begins to descend, with a wire fence on the right. Continue to follow the wire fence all the way down to its very end. Opposite to the end of the fence, look out for a sharp left-hand turn via a green metal barrier marked Winscombe and Sandford Award Land.

H Go through the barrier and along the path. After about 50 metres (beyond a seat), take the right hand turn down the steep path with a handrail. Take care –

this path can be awkward. At the T-junction at the bottom turn right. After about 50 metres go down left through the gate and continue to join a driveway. Follow the surfaced driveway downhill alongside the fence on the right. Bear left with the driveway at the bottom by the farm building and then turn right to join the main drive, which you follow all the way out on to the road. Turn right, following the road into Sandford. Cross the road junction and proceed straight ahead into Ilex Lane. After passing several dwellings off to the left, go over the stone bridge. Here immediately turn left to pick up the Strawberry Line path.

I You follow the Strawberry Line for most of the remainder of the walk. Proceed across various crossings and ignore various paths off to the left and right. Continue on past the old station. Just beyond here the facilities at Winscombe are indicated to the left (for which you may wish to make a detour). Continue on under a stone bridge, past the Winscombe Cricket Club on the left

and flights of steps on either side. After a seat on the right you reach a crossing track, which you traverse via succesive gates. About 300 metres on from here look out for steps with a wooden handrail off to the right.

J Take the steps up a bank and through the gate into Sladers Leigh, a local nature reserve. Turn left and proceed all the way up the narrow field. At the top go through a gate and descend to a T-junction with a wooded track. Turn left uphill on the track until you pass through a barrier to a road; you are now immediately opposite to the car park where you started. **A**

Crook Peak and Compton Bishop

Distance 6 miles / 9.5 kms

Time 3 to 3.5 hours

OS Map Explorer 153

Starting Point King's Wood National Trust car park, Winscombe Hill, off the A38 near Sidcot - OS reference 422560

Parking Free parking at King's Wood car park

Reaching the start from Bristol Take the A38 south out of Bristol and beyond the airport and Churchill. About a mile beyond the centre of Sidcot, over the brow of a hill and immediately after a filling station look out for a turning off to the right. Take the lane and the car park is immediately visible off to the left

Refreshments A short detour to the New Inn or the White Hart in Cross

---

THIS DRAMATIC West Mendip walk, mainly on tracks and paths, focuses on Crook Peak, the only pointed peak on the Mendip Hills. On route it also explores nearby King's Wood, Wavering Down, Barton Drove and Compton Bishop, all of which are worth visiting in their own right. Although this is one of the shortest walks in the book, it is somewhat strenuous, with much uphill walking, including two or three steep stretches and one long prolonged descent. In the right weather conditions, however, you will be richly rewarded with spectacular vistas covering a very wide panorama.

The walk starts with an uphill climb through the ancient King's Wood, known for its diversity of lime trees. The West Mendip Way soon emerges on to the open land of Wavering Down where the views begin to open up. The route diverts downhill to follow the ancient Barton Drove on a varied hillside route with views to the north. Eventually there is a dramatic climb back uphill to reconnect with Wavering Down. You continue on the West Mendip Way again in the direction of Crook Peak, eventually climbing it. There follows a long steady ridge descent to reach the village of Compton Bishop. After this, there is a flat stretch traversing numerous fields, before you reach a disused quarry and then re-enter woodland. Ultimately the route re-enters King's Wood and you briefly retrace your earliest steps back to the car park.

A Enter King's Wood via the gate at the far end of the car park. Immediately climb uphill on the broad track – the West Mendip Way. As you climb up through the woodland, keep within no more than 50 metres or so from the wall away on your right. You emerge from the woodland into open land. Keep on in the same direction, staying with the wall immediately on your right, as the terrain eventually levels out. Continue until you reach Hill Farm off to the right. Take a gate to turn right near a waymark post, immediately past the farmhouse.

B Go ahead through the farmyard. Take the gate out of the farm straight downhill on the stony and then surfaced track for about 250 metres until you reach a T-junction. Turn left on to Barton Drove, which you will now be following for about 800 metres. Keep with the stony track as it rises gently and levels out and passes in and out of woodland. Pass Old Quarry Farm on the left. Here, continue ahead through a gate as the track becomes grassy. Go through a gate to enter a copse, after which the track becomes more of a path. Continue through the copse and exit via a further gate to enter a field. Keep to the left edge of the field, which abuts woodland, and pass a redundant stile. Then cross the open field downhill to take a further stile. Enter a fenced/wooded path. Follow the path uphill through woodland, as it passes to the left of a house and narrows. Upon exiting woodland stick with the now hedged path, which eventually descends to reach a stile.

C Take the stile and then immediately turn left to climb steeply up the track. Immediately the track reaches trees take the right-hand fork. Follow the track uphill to reach open land. Here the paths are a little confusing. You need to bear slightly right on a poorly-defined path towards and through a row of trees ahead. Having passed through the trees, look to your right and you will see a gate in a wall. Take the well-defined path

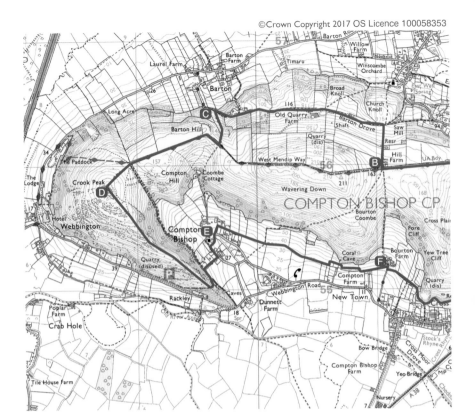

© Crown Copyright 2017 OS Licence 100058353

towards and through the gate to re-join the West Mendip Way. Turn right and keep with the wall on your right for a long distance as you head in the direction of Crook Peak, which should be visible ahead. Keep with the wall all the way down to where it ends, near to a waymark post. Here take the track straight ahead to ascend Crook Peak. When you near the top, bear very slightly right and then back upon yourself to scramble up to the peak.

D From the peak, facing towards Brent Knoll and the M5 in its southerly direction, turn left to descend straight down the grassy ridge. The footpath is not always distinct but essentially you keep along the grassy ridge as it descends and gradually narrows. Persist with the ridge for as long as possible, with the vista of Cheddar reservoir and Glastonbury Tor ahead of you (on a clear day at least) and the village of Compton Bishop down to your left. Soon after reaching woodland off to the left, you reach a wooden barrier ahead. Go through the barrier and immediately turn sharp left to take a path down into the woodland. As the path nears a wall to the right, ignore a turning off to the left. Continue ahead with the wall on your right. Go through a field gate and down a sunken track/lane to enter the village of Compton Bishop. At the road junction turn left. Pass the old Manor House and curve

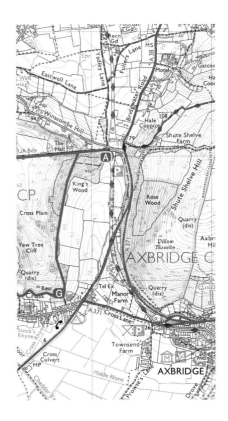

rightwards down Church Lane in front of St Andrew's Church, which is of 13th century origin. At the end of Church Lane, cross straight ahead.

E Take the surfaced track and keep with it as it bends round to the right and then goes through a stable yard. Take the stile and proceed in the field with the hedge on your right. Cross a stile and go through a further field and a gate. The next field is a long one but you still stick with the right-hand boundary. Cross a stile and go through two further fields and across further stiles, keeping in parallel with Wavering Down up on your left, again sticking closely to the right-hand hedge. At the end of the second field, go ahead through the gap, ignoring a track off to the right. In the next field continue ahead, still boundary right, until reaching a garden and house ahead. Here divert round to the left and right, following the boundary and then cross a stile in the fence ahead. Go down the centre of the next field to cross another stile. In the following field continue in the same direction, keeping to the right-hand hedgerow and then an embankment to take a stile to the right of a farm ahead.

F Cross the drive and head up a bank to take the stile ahead into a field. Keep with the right-hand boundary of the field. Go through a gate to enter another field. In the next field again keep to the right-hand boundary and enter a further small field via a gap in the hedge. From here continue in the same direction and go through a further gate in the corner. In the following field continue with the hedge until its corner, at which point you bear right across the field to take a metal gate in the far boundary. You enter a former quarry and scrubland. Carry on ahead, keeping the wall to your right. Ignore a path off to the right and continue to follow the wall as long as you can. Keep with the well-defined path that climbs and contours the rocky/grassy/scrubby slopes. Eventually the now undulating path approaches woodland. On entering the fringes of the woodland you almost immediately reach a crossroads of paths.

G At this junction you turn left (although you can detour here by turning right and going downhill for about 200 metres to reach the main village street in

Cross, where there are pubs, and then return to the junction by the same route). From the junction, climb uphill for about 200 metres until the path levels out. You eventually reach and follow the right-hand edge of the woodland. Carry on with the path as it gently descends again towards a wooden field gate. Go through the gate to re-enter King's Wood. Continue on the now broader path, still adjacent to the right-hand boundary. Just before reaching the end of the adjacent long open field below, look out for a waymark post ahead. Here, bear left uphill for about 10 metres to fork on to a parallel path climbing gently uphill. Proceed on this path for about 200 metres until you reach a small gate. Go through this and ahead for about a further 50 metres to reach a T-junction. You should recognise this as you will have passed it at the beginning of the walk, on the West Mendip Way. Turn right and retrace your steps downhill to reach the car park and your starting point. **A**

Hinton Charterhouse and Midford

Distance 8 miles / 13 kms

Time 4 to 4.5 hours

OS Map Explorer 142 and 155

Starting Point St John the Baptist Church, Green Lane, Hinton Charterhouse - OS reference 776583

Parking Free on-road parking in the vicinity of the church

Reaching the start from Bristol Head for Bath on the A4. Go through Saltford and at the Globe Inn take the road for Newton St Loe that goes on to skirt Bath via Odd Down. At Odd Down pick up the B3110. Go through Midford to reach Hinton Charterhouse. Immediately after the Rose and Crown turn left and continue for 200 metres

Refreshments The Rose and Crown or the Stag, Hinton Charterhouse, the Wheatsheaf, Combe Hay or the Hope and Anchor, Midford

---

THIS WALK explores the kaleidoscope of rolling hills, valleys, streams and villages that characterise the area immediately to the south of Bath. There is archaeological and historic interest on route; especially the disused Somerset Coal Canal. The terrain is undulating with a long climb towards the end. There are some muddy patches.

From Hinton Charterhouse the walk descends steeply through open fields and woodland to cross the **Wellow Brook** and go under the former railway now used as a cycle path. The route wends back uphill and through the hamlet of Middle Twinhoe. You descend further through woodland to reach a notable weir and cross the Cam Brook at Combe Hay. You then ascend the opposite side of the valley via Rowley Farm before descending again to follow a tributary brook and the line of the old canal. You continue from here with the canal and eventually the Cam Brook again all the way to Midford, where you pass beneath a spectacular viaduct and by an historic water mill with a further weir. From here the route wends steadily uphill again on a wooded track, with distant views of Midford Castle. At Pipehouse the route deviates back towards Hinton Charterhouse, skirting Hinton Abbey Priory. St John the Baptist Church appears ahead on the horizon. You go through the churchyard to return to the start.

alongside through the woodland for about 100 metres. Take a wooden footbridge on the left, which leads towards a larger metal footbridge, which you also take to cross a larger stream. At the end of the metal footbridge take a gate to exit the woodland and enter a field. In the field turn right and keep to the right-hand boundary until reaching a metal field gate. Cross this to take a hedged/fenced track which climbs steeply upwards. You go under a redundant railway viaduct, beneath what is now a cycle path. Continue uphill on the track. When you reach a house immediately ahead, take a track off to the left.

C Keep with the hedged track as it proceeds uphill into a cutting, running along the left-hand edge of a field, into which it eventually emerges in the top corner. Here go through the gap into the next field, where you continue straight ahead across the field in the same direction and through a gate in the hedge. In the following field keep ahead to take a field gate just to the right of a barn, attached to a dwelling. Turn right down the driveway to the road. Cross the road and turn right for about 30 metres until on the left you reach a waymarked footpath through a field gate. Go over the gate to take this footpath and proceed diagonally across the long narrow field to take a gate in far right-hand corner. In the next field a lake is visible over to the right. Bear slightly right down the field, aiming immediately for the double field gates evident in the hedge ahead.

A From the church go back down Green Lane towards the village centre. At the main road turn right by the Rose and Crown public house. After the bus shelter cross the road. Proceed ahead past the Stag public house. Take the Wellow Road off to the left and follow it for no more than 30 metres, before taking the lane going down to the right. Keep with the lane, ignoring paths off to the left and right, as it gradually descends towards houses which come into view ahead. Follow the path between the houses through a gate and into a large field.

B Head down the field, keeping towards the right-hand boundary. Go through a gate into another field and then down via a gap into a further field, still keeping to the right edge. The third field funnels down towards a gate leading into woodland. Enter the woodland. Take the path ahead and follow it as it veers right to cross the stream via a bridge. With the stream now on your left, follow the path

D Go through the gate across a lane, through another gate immediately opposite and into a large field. Proceed on the track with the field boundary on your left. Stick with the left-hand boundary as it curves round to the left. At the corner

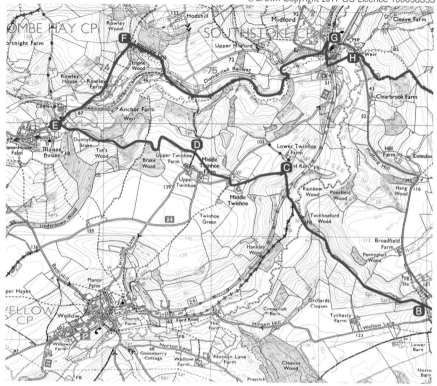

turn right and proceed with the left-hand boundary, still in the field but now alongside woodland. At the end of this woodland, continue in the same direction through a gate indicating that you are now in a Conservation Area. Briefly pass through another field, before descending into scrubby woodland. Keep with the same track, which is muddy in places, as it gradually descends. The track becomes enclosed between woodland and a field boundary. Carefully follow the waymarks until you eventually pass through a field gate into open land. In the field keep downhill with the right-hand boundary to exit via a gate and re-enter woodland. From here the now fenced track continues down towards an impressive weir and then curves right to cross the Cam Brook. Go ahead past farm buildings on the right to reach an exit on to the road.

E At the road turn right uphill, passing a mail box on your right and the Wheatsheaf Inn on your left. You soon reach a road junction. Here bear left on the no through road. Keep uphill towards Rowley Farm, through which you pass, carefully following the footpath signs. Keep ahead, passing Rowley Farm House and associated holiday cottages on your right. Stick with the driveway as it morphs into a farm track and goes through a copse, passing Rowley Farm Stables on the left. Beyond the copse continue ahead until you reach a field gate ahead. Here go down to the right via steps to take the kissing gate into a field. Proceed diagonally left down the field

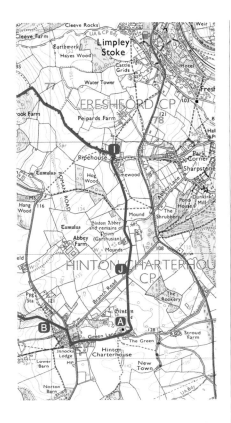

about a further 200 metres. You go through a wooded area and eventually reach a junction of paths via a gate. Here turn right and proceed for about 10 metres before taking the gate to your left. Go through the gate and down the steps. Continue in the same direction as before. You are still following the route of the disused canal via its towpath but the canal is now on your left-hand side; with a much more open vista ahead and the river evident over to your right. Keep to the towpath as it wends left and right, passing through a gate, a stile and another gate near to a viaduct. Follow the path round to the right as it reaches the river and then curves through the viaduct. After this the path curves left and through another gate with a derelict canal bridge appearing off to the left. From here follow the path round to the right and through another gate. Then continue along the embankment. Soon after entering scrubland, go through another gate. Climb uphill on the fenced path and beneath a viaduct to eventually emerge up steps to Midford; immediately opposite to the Hope and Anchor public house and by a canal bridge on the B3110 road.

G Here turn left, go under the viaduct again and then turn immediately left down a lane. Continue for about 100 metres, adjacent to the viaduct and cross two bridges before taking the left turn. Pass beneath the viaduct (yet again) to go through the gate straight ahead, with the river now on your left. In the field follow the alignment of the low embankment immediately to your right. Head in the direction of a footbridge and an old watermill ahead. Go through a gate, cross the footbridge and reach the B3110 road once again. Turn left along the road for about 50 metres. Cross to pick up a well-defined track opposite.

and through a gate in the corner. In the next field continue more steeply down the valley via scrub, curving to the right to enter woodland at the bottom. Cross the shallow stream via stepping stones to join a footpath on the other side.

F You now turn right to pick up the route of the former Somerset Coal Canal. Within 50 metres go through a gate and continue straight ahead. You keep ahead on the path through scrubby woodland, passing a series of disused lock chambers off to your right. Eventually you reach a stile, which you cross to reach a viaduct. Go under the viaduct and through a gate leading out to a road. Cross the road and go through another gate. Pick up and follow the fenced-in path (which can be very muddy) for

H Proceed steeply uphill on the wooded and wending track which has been recently resurfaced, although it remains rough and rocky in places. Stick with this track, from which in due course there are regular glimpses of Midford Castle and Midford village off to the left; particularly at the point at which it bends sharply to the right. From this sharp bend persist uphill with this same wooded track. Continue on with it for about a further 1000 metres as it curves right and the gradient levels. Eventually the track morphs into a road and approaches Pipehouse. Ignore the path off to the right as you reach the edge of the hamlet. Proceed into the built up area and look out on each side of the road for the signage of a crossing footpath between the houses.

I Take the right-hand turn, immediately before Ashleigh Cottage. Proceed along the narrow hedged footpath. Go through a gate and across two sets of stiles in close succession to enter a narrow field, with farm buildings off to your left. Cross a stile in the right-hand corner to enter another field. Keep to the right-hand hedge and go through a gate, with the remains of Hinton Abbey priory now visible ahead of you through the trees. In the following field continue in the same direction to cross a stile. In the next field, keep to the right of the buildings ahead, going through a gate. Keep ahead on the path next to the boundary adjacent with the woodland of the priory grounds. Proceed through another gate. Continue similarly in the following field in parallel with the edge of the priory grounds. Go through a further gate in the far boundary into a further field. Bear half-right across the field to take a gate on to a busy road.

J Cross the road to enter a gate into a field opposite. Go up the field and through a further gate in the far boundary. Now head uphill in the direction of a prominent group of trees, to the left of Hinton Charterhouse church, which comes increasingly into view. You are aiming for a small gate into the churchyard, situated about 100 metres to the left of the church itself. Take the gate to enter the churchyard and follow the path alongside the wall. Pass the church and exit via the main churchyard entrance. You have reached the start. **A**

Priddy and Wookey Hole

Distance 10 miles / 16 kms

Time 5 to 5.5 hours

OS Map Explorer 141

Starting Point South-east corner of Priddy Green, Priddy - OS reference 527509

Parking Free on or near to Priddy Green

Reaching the start from Bristol Take the A37 Wells Road through Farrington Gurney and Chewton Mendip. Just after passing through a set of traffic lights, look out for the right-hand turn signed to Priddy. Continue straight along this lane for about three miles to reach Priddy Green

Refreshments Queen Victoria, Priddy and various options at Wookey Hole

THIS IS A CLASSIC Mendip walk on field paths, drove roads and quiet lanes, encompassing spectacular panoramic views, nature reserves, woodland and a variety of historical interest and archaeology. The walk starts in Priddy, the highest village on Mendip, and features the notable Ebbor Gorge. There is one steep descent, down to Ebbor Gorge, and then a strenuous ascent back up to the Mendip ridge.

The walk exits the village by a quiet lane and then proceeds across fields and open access towards Deer Leap, where there are panoramic views across the Somerset Levels. From here the route briefly picks up the ancient Dursdon Drove before diverging towards Ebbor Nature Reserve, where there are further panoramic views. After descending into Ebbor Gorge you go through the village of Wookey Hole, passing the caves. From here it is a steep climb up the escarpment; well rewarded though by yet more long distance views. Back at the top of Mendip, a long straight path leads eventually to the former Priddy Minories mine workings and nature reserve. Beyond here the path curves up towards and via three groupings of Bronze-Age barrows. A quiet lane takes you past Priddy Pool and a detour via St Lawrence's Church returns you to Priddy Green.

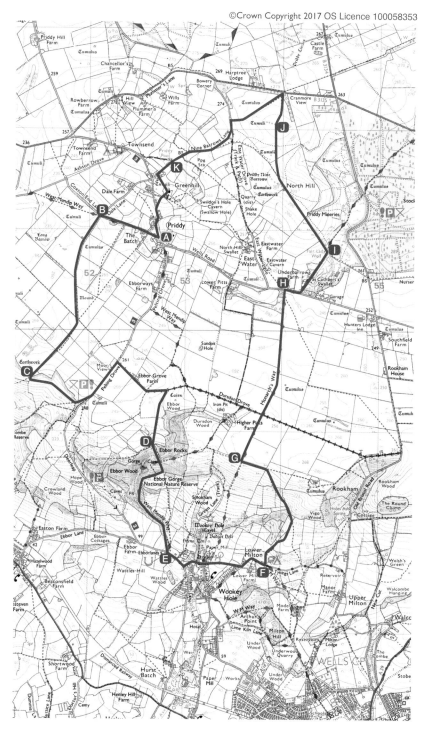

A The walk starts on the south-eastern corner of Priddy Green, adjacent to the bus shelter/village notice board and the public telephone box, now in use as a defibrillator. With the telephone box on your left proceed ahead along the southern edge of the green. At the end of the green continue in the same direction following the lane marked to Draycott as it rises gently uphill and levels out. Continue along the lane until you reach another lane coming in from the right.

B Take the stile/gate in the wall opposite to enter the field. Follow the track ahead by the left-hand wall. In the corner of the field cross a stone stile into another field. Continue with the left-hand boundary of this field as the path gradually curves around to the left. In the corner you take successive wooden and stone stiles into the next field. Continue with the left-hand boundary until in the corner you go through a metal gate and immediately cross a stone stile into a further field. Go left for about 10 metres to pick up a crossing path. Turn right adjacent to a stone stile and head across the field to take another stone stile. Proceed in the same direction across another field to cross a further stone stile. In the next field, as views of the Somerset Levels open up ahead, keep to the left-hand wall and follow this until you reach a stile and information board about Cook's Field Nature Reserve. Do not take the stile immediately ahead.

C Instead take the stone stile immediately to your left to enter open access land. Take the track ahead and continue with the wall away on your left. When the track forks keep to the left uphill. Go through a gate in the left-hand corner, leading into the Deer Leap car park and picnic area. From the gate turn left to follow the path along left-hand boundary

wall until you reach the road. Proceed along the road for about 400 metres. Just after passing Moor View Cottage on your left, you reach a track on your right. Take this ancient track, Dursdon Drove. Pass the farm on the left to reach a metal gate ahead. Do not take this but follow the track for about a further 200 metres as it curves round to the left. Then just before a field boundary off to the right, look out for a hidden stile in the hedgerow. Take the stile to enter the field. In the field go ahead keeping near but not directly adjacent to the left-hand hedge of the field. Bear left and uphill to cross a stile in the stone wall ahead. Continue straight ahead in a similar direction in the next field towards a gap by a waymark post, with woodland both ahead and away to your left. Go through the gap. In the next field bear right towards the woodland ahead to take a stile in a fence.

D Turn left for about 50 metres to reach an entrance to Ebbor Gorge Nature Reserve. Cross the stile to enter woodland. Descend steeply on the sometimes slippery path until you reach a junction of paths. Go straight ahead uphill to reach a further crossing path. Here turn right and follow the path for about 150 metres, ignoring (for now) a path off to your left, until you reach a cliff-edge where there is a spectacular view. Retrace your steps for about 50 metres back to the footpath that you just ignored, now on your right. Take this path and follow the many steps downhill, sticking with the stony path as it meanders down through the woodland to eventually reach a junction with a crossing track at the bottom of the gorge. Turn left and proceed for about 150 metres to take a gate/stile to exit both the woodland and the Reserve. From here, continue along a grassy track within the wooded valley

until a house appears straight ahead, on the edge of the village of Wookey Hole. Keep with the track as it funnels to the right of the bungalow towards a metal gate and out on to a road.

E Turn left and walk down the road to the centre of Wookey Hole. Pass the path to the caves on your left and the pay booth and hotel on your right. Within about 100 metres of doing so, look out as the main road bends to the right and School Lane appears up to your left. You need to take the footpath immediately ahead of you up the concrete steps. Climb a tarmac path that leads up to a gate, with cottages up to your left. Go through the gate and across a stone stile. In the field proceed along the right-hand hedge to go through a field gate. In the next field follow the track ahead in the same direction, keeping to the left of the houses at the top, to go through a metal gate in the right-hand corner and steps down to a lane. Turn left and uphill along the lane, passing Myrtle Farm on the left. Keep with the lane as it meanders. Ignore a turn off to the right and

continue for about a further 100 metres until you reach a derelict cottage on the left. Immediately adjacent to the bottom of the garden of the cottage you reach a metal field gate, with a 'no parking' sign attached.

F Take the gate and walk up the field, keeping to the right-hand hedge. At the top right-hand corner, go through a gate to pick up a track which continues uphill, with the hedge now to your left. Go through another gate. Follow the track up the next field, keeping near to the left-hand hedge. Continue uphill to the top left-hand corner of the field towards a gate. Go through this gate to enter woodland. Continue up the track. You then pass through a metal gate to exit the woodland and enter an open field. Keep uphill with the hedge and trees towards your right and continue uphill on what becomes a path through scrubland. Eventually you go through a gate/stile ahead to reach a large open field. In the field continue uphill in a similar direction, bearing gently left. Look for a metal gate in the boundary

about 100 metres before the far corner. Cross the stile next to the gate to enter another field. Go ahead for about 200 metres with the wall on your right until you reach a wooden stile in the wall in the far corner.

G Turn right to take the stile. You now simply keep to the left-hand boundary of the next six fields, crossing Dursdon Drove (again) and various stiles on route, as you eventually descend to gate leading on to a road.

H At the road turn right and pass three cottages on the left. At the side of the third cottage go left along the drive to Underbarrow Farm. At the fork bear left into the yard of a caving centre. Aim for the far right-hand corner to exit via a stile. Then cross the drive and a further stile to enter Priddy Minories Nature Reserve. Here you follow a grassy path between trees and remnants of former lead workings, keeping within no more than about 50 metres of a wall running to your left. Carry on ahead through the scrubby woodland until you reach a waymark post next to a clump of beech trees. In the same vicinity the wall that you have been following comes to a corner and a pond becomes evident off to the right.

I Take the path that leads off to the left beyond the wall corner. Keep with the wall on your left as you proceed uphill through long grass, crossing various small ditches on the way. Eventually in the top left-hand corner you reach a stile. Cross the stile to leave the reserve. In the field keep with the wall on your left as you continue to climb gently to the top of the hill. You pass the concrete cap of an underground reservoir and then seven tumuli on your left, with a further two down the hill ahead. Look half-right and you will see another row of eight tumuli, towards which you will shortly be heading. From the top of the hill keep with the wall for about a further 100 metres until you reach a waymark post in the wall. From here strike out half right to take a visible stile in the fence.

Enter the large field and keep going in the same direction towards the centre of the row of tumuli.

J Your next manoeuvre from here is complicated. Look ahead to the right-hand corner of the field and proceed directly ahead towards the field gate, which is the obvious exit point on to the main road. Once you have reached the gate, do not go through it. Instead stay within the field and check the waymark sign pointing leftwards across the field. As waymarked, turn back diagonally left across the field, initially in the direction of a telegraph pole, with the tumuli now on your left and the main road away to your right. When you have reached the telegraph pole, take a bearing at least 100 metres to the left of the line of conifers on the horizon. Continue past the conifers and head towards the far right-hand corner of this very large field. Eventually look out for a small wooden gate in the right-hand boundary about 100 metres short of the far right-hand corner. Exit the gate. Ignore a track off

to the left. Instead turn left along the tarmac lane. Keep on the lane to reach Priddy Pool on your right.

K Beyond Priddy Pool, continue on the lane uphill for about a further 200 metres. Look out for a track off to the left, opposite to the first house you reach on the right. Take the walled drive and go through a field gate. Proceed on the track across the field to enter Priddy churchyard via a further gate. Skirt round to the right of the church. Leave the churchyard via a fenced path with two closely-spaced gates, to reach a lane with the primary school and village hall to your left. Turn right and then immediately left downhill, with the wall on your left. The lane joins with a road coming in from the right. Here turn left. Within about 100 metres you reach Priddy Green. The Queen Victoria is just beyond the far end of the green, where you started the walk. **A**

Photo: Lara Tetlow

Robin Tetlow was born and brought up in the Midlands, eventually moving to Bristol in 1986. He is a chartered surveyor and town planner specialising in housing, and co-founder of Tetlow King Planning.

Robin has had a life-long interest in walking, travel and the natural environment. These 24 walks are simply his favourites based on more than 30 years of exploring the country around Bristol.